Elvan Ece Satıcı

Ece is a recent graduate from the Robert College of Istanbul and is an upcoming freshman at Yale University. She started as a volunteer at Good4Trust.org in 2020, working for Dr. Özesmi. Later, her volunteering endeavors turned into part-time employment at Good4Trust.org in 2021. She is the Field Generator and Management Circle Coordinator at Good4trust.org. As an Associate, she carried out a supply network modelling project and handled internationalization processes. She also co-authored an article on Arxiv.org on the Environmental Kuznets Curve and the effectiveness of international policies, besides the Turkish Edition of the *Prosumer Economy* book.

Uygar Özesmi

Dr. Özesmi is an environmental scientist, and an Ashoka Senior Fellow. He has a masters in Environmental Science from Ohio State University as a Fulbright Scholar, a PhD as a MacArthur Scholar in Conservation Biology, as well as in Development and Social Change at the University of Minnesota. He founded the Environmental Engineering Department at Erciyes University, where he was Asst. Professor and Chair of Environmental Science (2000-2004). He founded the first crowd-sourcing site and citizen-science project in Turkey called KusBank.org in 2001. Uygar was also the founding chairperson of Doğa Derneği (BirdLife Partner) in 2002. He then joined the United Nations Development Program in New York as Environmental Specialist (2004-2006). He served as the Executive Director of TEMA Foundation (2006-2008) and Greenpeace Mediterranean (2008-2012). He founded Change.org in Turkey in 2012 and still is the Executive Director. He is a founding member of the Civil Society Development Center (STGM) and served for two terms on the Board of CIVICUS – World Alliance for Citizen Participation. He also currently serves on the Board of Ashoka and ENIVA Foundation. He is the founder and instigator of Good4Trust.org, an online system for creating a prosumer economy for ecological and social sustainability. He is the board chair of the Prosumer Economy Association. He is Adjunct Asst. Professor at Kadir Has University teaching Sustainable Energy and also Ecological Economics. He has more than 100 scientific publications, countless popular articles, two books, and has a daily radio program at Açık Radio.

THE PROSUMER ECONOMY
Being Like a Forest

Ece Satıcı and Uygar Özesmi

Dixi Books
Copyright © 2024 by Ece Satıcı and Uygar Özesmi
Copyright © 2024 by Dixi Books
All rights reserved. No part of this book may be used or reproduced or transmitted to any form or by any means, electronic or mechanical, including photocopying, recording, or by any information and retrieval system, without written permission from the Publisher.

The Prosumer Economy
Ece Satıcı and Uygar Özesmi
Editor: Zadie Loft
Designer: Pablo Ulyanov
Cover Design: Efdal Basan
I. Edition: March 2024

Library of Congress Cataloging-in-Publication Data
ISBN: 978-1-913680-93-0
1. Ecology 2. Adult Non-Fiction 3. Economy 4. Sustainability
5. Prosumerism

© Dixi Books Publishing
293 Green Lanes, Palmers Green, London, N13 4XS, England
info@dixibooks.com
www.dixibooks.com

THE PROSUMER ECONOMY
Being Like a Forest

Ece Satıcı and Uygar Özesmi

The Voice of the New Age

Table of Contents

Preface 9
Is Gaia Getting Rid of Us? 13
    The Ecological Cost of Consumption 18
    The Social Cost of Consumption 19
Demands for Change 23
Reform and Change Efforts 29
    Seeking a Technological Fix 29
    Corporate Social Responsibility 30
    Polluter Pays Principle 32
    Value-Based Approach - Creating Value for Stakeholders ... 35
    Degrowth 36
    Solidarity Economy 41
    Commons Movement and a Critique of Companies 43
    P2P 45
    Social Enterprises 47
    Transition Network 49
The Prosumer Economy: The Anatomy of Transformation 51
    The Transition to the Prosumer Economy 55
    Regeneration After Transitioning to the Prosumer
    Economy 60

Being Like a Forest 61
Putting the Prosumer Economy into Practice: Good4Trust 65
    Governance in Good4Trust 71
    Good4Trust in Operation and Growing 74
The Challenges Faced by the Prosumer Economy 79
Is the Prosumer Economy the Future? 81
References 83

PREFACE

Planetary life support systems are collapsing due to climate change and the biodiversity crisis. We have very little time. If current trends continue, human civilisation is facing collapse within the next 30 to 40 years. The root cause is the existing consumer economy, coupled with profit maximisation based on ecological and social externalities.

However, this trend can be reversed. With careful examination, we can see glimmers of hope all around us. These glimmers of hope include not only white-collar workers trying to buy organic products, but also the efforts of people outside their personal lives to make their own companies carbon neutral. There is also an increase in the number of people who define themselves as social entrepreneurs, focusing on ecologically and socially fair production, rather than only entrepreneurs. These conscious, devoted people show all kinds of effort, and their numbers are increasing day by day. It is not only the individuals that are transforming; the reasons for the existence of companies and their legal entity rights are also being questioned now. It is said that a company should increase its impact, rather than its profits. The glimmers of hope are growing brighter.

Civilisation may be saved by transforming the profit-maximising consumer economy into an ecologically and socially just economy, which we call "the Prosumer Economy." The Prosumer Economy is a macroscale circular economy with positive, or just minimum negative, ecological and social impact. It is an ecosystem of producers and prosumers,[1] who have synergistic and circular relationships with deepened circular supply chains/networks, where leakage of wealth out of the system is minimised. In a prosumer economy, there is no waste, no lasting negative impacts on the ecology, and no social exploitation. The prosumer economy is like a lake or a forest, an economic ecosystem that is productive and supportive of the planet. This system is not a dream anymore, it is real.

We are already planting this forest through Good4Trust, which was started in Turkey in 2014. Good4Trust is a community, bringing together ecologically and socially just producers and prosumers. Prosumers come together around the basic ethical tenet of "the golden rule" and share their good deeds on the platform. These good deeds may include charity, volunteering, or supporting ecologically and socially just production. Prosumers purchase goods and services on the Good4Trust online bazaar to support production and the continuity of the Prosumer Economy. As these prosumer relationships deepen and become circular, the Prosumer Economy starts to form. To help the growth of the Prosumer Economy, the platform's software is open-source and available to be licensed to start Good4Trust anywhere on the planet.

Complexity theory tells us that if enough agents in a given system adopt simple rules which they all follow, the system may shift. The shift from a consumer economy to a Prosumer Economy has already started, the future is either ecologically and socially just, or bust. This book was written to prevent us from going bust and to establish an economic ecosystem where humans can exist in harmony with the planet, just like a forest.

Many people inspired us to write the book. Neşet Kutluğ was always there with Uygar from the days of Greenpeace to Good-

---

1   A prosumer is a person who treats others in the way that they want to be treated themselves, creating value for the society and the planet through their actions. They directly support socially and ecologically just production. Prosumers decide on the goods, the services, and their standards with the producers, as a community. Prosumers do not only purchase from them, but also take an active role in their relationships with the producers.

4Trust's founding, a major source of inspiration and support. Our teammates at Good4Trust, volunteers and members of the 7's Council, Paradigm Change Working Group (2009-12) and Eco Eco Thinking Group (2011), Michael Narberhaus, Greenpeace, David Fell and all SmartCSO members, Burcu Tuncer, Gülcan Nitsch, Ümit Şahin, Ömer Madra, Ashoka Foundation Turkey and Ashoka Fellows, Sibel Asna, Selin Gücüm, Ece Yener, Buket Uzuner, Doğa Özesmi, Aynur Satıcı, and Emine Doğrukök have all contributed in many ways. Thank you all.

Is Gaia Getting Rid of Us?

Scientists state that since 1980, the Earth has surpassed its capacity to renew itself. According to the Intergovernmental Panel on Climate Change, the biggest problem facing humanity is the climate emergency, which could cause an irreversible ecological and social catastrophe if the global average temperature increases by more than 2°C (IPCC, 2018). This could lead to the collapse of civilisation as we know it.

The level of carbon dioxide in the atmosphere before industrialisation was 280 parts per million (ppm). In January 2022, at the Mauna Loa Station of the US National Oceanic and Atmospheric Administration in Hawaii, this concentration was measured to be 418 ppm[2] (NOAA Global Monitoring Laboratory). Hansen et al. suggests that, "in order to preserve a planet similar to that on which civilization developed" CO_2 will need to be reduced to at most 350 ppm (13). The fact that the level of the carbon dioxide in the atmosphere has surpassed 350 ppm shows that we have exceeded the safe limit. This 350 ppm limit was broken for the first time in January 1988. The level of carbon dioxide concentration before the industrial era had not surpassed 300 ppm for 800 thousand years. *Homo sapiens* evolved in this period and has been on Earth for about 300,000 years. Human activity has increased average temperatures probably in the range of 0.8°C to 1.2°C since the Industrial Revolution. By crossing the 400 ppm carbon dioxide concentration, we have increased the average temperature by 1.1°C (IPCC 4). If temperatures continue to rise at the current rate, global warming is likely to reach 1.5-2.0°C between

---

[2] Please see https://gml.noaa.gov/ccgg/trends/ for the latest measurements.

2030 and 2052 (IPCC 4). An average increase of 1°C may not seem like much; however, 1°C corresponds to an increase of 7 to 15°C in extreme weather conditions (Fang et al. 1-8). Scientists state that, in the 21st century, there have been widespread and persistent changes in extreme air temperature much earlier than expected (Fang et al. 1).

To illustrate this, let's look at an example from Turkey. Turkish State Meteorology Agency data show that between 15-19 February 2016 in Milas, Muğla the temperature was 32.4°C; whereas, before, the highest ever recorded February temperature was 24.9°C in 1950 (MGM). In other words, there was a difference of 7.5°C in extreme temperatures.

Let's go beyond Turkey and examine extreme temperatures measured in 2020 around the world: The highest temperatures recorded in 2020 were 37°C in London (UK), 40°C in Paris (France), 36°C in New York (USA), 41.1°C in Hamamatsu (Japan), and 49.4°C in Los Angeles (USA).

Let's assume a 1.1°C increase in the temperature, which is more than 7°C in extreme weather, just like in Milas, Muğla. If we don't change our way of consumption and use of products such as coal, oil, natural gas, and other fossil fuels, the temperature would increase 2.6 – 3.2°C by 2050 (Brown and Caldeira 45-50). So, we are foreseeing about 15°C additionally in the extremes... So, let's add 15°C to see what extreme temperatures we would expect in 2050: London 52°C, Paris 54°C, New York 51°C, Hamamatsu 56.1°C, and Los Angeles 64.4°C. In a conservative scenario, Bador et al. estimate temperatures exceeding 50°C in France in 2100 (10). Probably by 2050, or more cautiously by 2100, these temperatures may be fatal for humanity. Unfortunately, global warming is happening at an ever increasing rate (Xu et al. 30). Indeed, on July 19th, 2022, the temperature in Paris reached 40.5°C (Desai).

As another example, in July 2022 one of London Heathrow Airport's runways melted due to extreme heat and was closed to flights (Vera). Furthermore, Hammersmith Bridge was covered with silver foil to protect it from extreme heat and some railways were painted white (Vera). In fact, on July 19th, 2022, the temperature in London reached 40.2°C; whereas, the previous highest temperature in July was 36.1°C in 2019 (Kirk et al.). Also in July 2022, extreme heat melted the roof of the Forbidden City Cultural Relics Museum in China and burst water pipes on several trunk lines in Texas (Vera). In India, the hottest day of 2022 was on May 14, 2022, when the temperature reached 44.2°C in Delhi (Vera). Furthermore, India experienced a total of 203 heat waves (28 in Uttarakhand, 26 in Rajasthan, 24 each in Punjab and Haryana, 18 in Jharkhand, and 17 in Delhi, etc.) until the end of July in 2022, which is 5 times more compared to previous years (Mohan). According to Effis data, there were over 515,000 hectares of land that were burnt due to the fires in European Union countries on July 23–4 times the average fire area since 2006 and 2 times the previous record fire area in this period (Kirk et al.). It is horrifying to even predict the temperatures that will be experienced in 2050 if global warming continues to increase at this rate.

To avert the collapse of civilisation, the success of The United Nations Framework Convention of Climate Change (UNFCCC) is critical, but progress is slow, and the threat is fast and horrifying. Unfortunately, governments and political leaders are still not facing this huge issue. Climate change leads to storms and floods, as well as droughts, causing a freshwater crisis. This will result in agricultural collapse and hygiene problems. If global warming continues to increase at this rate, humanity will face widespread famine and disease. At extreme temperatures, roads and cables may melt, and the Earth may no longer be habitable. Quite a dystopia… So, what's the solution? Before we move onto the solution, we need to clarify another great threat.

Biological diversity is the diversity of living beings, including humans, and their habitats. It is also defined by the diversity of the relations among living beings and their environment. This diversity is disappearing today. According to the report of WWF in 2020, populations of vertebrate animals—such as mammals, birds, and fish—have declined by 68% between 1970 and 2020 (WWF and ZSL 6). Humans and domesticated animals make up 97% of the world's animal population by mass, while wildlife only makes up 3% (MacCready 227-233)

Currently, out of 149 million km^2 of total land area on the planet, including deserts and glaciers, we have transformed 51 million km^2 into agriculture. Of the habitable area, 50% is used for humans (Figure 1). Out of the agricultural areas, 77% is used to grow feed for animals which we have domesticated. With the remaining 23%, we feed ourselves. This 77% agricultural land allocated to animal feed only constitutes 17% of human calorie intake and 33% of protein intake. While the rest of the 83% of calories and 67% of protein needed for human consumption are produced on 23% of the available agricultural land. Livestock takes up nearly 80% of global agricultural land, yet produces less than 20% of the world's supply of calories (Ritchie).

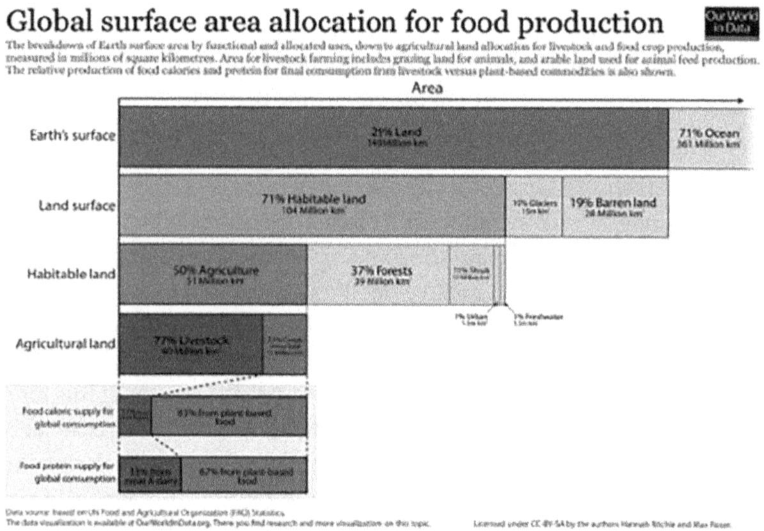

Figure 1: *Global surface allocation for human use (Richie and Roser)*

With this level of terrestrial human invasion, we have destroyed the habitats of other large animals on land. Also marine ecosystems and fish populations are suffering drastic damage, and many marine animals are threatened. Data from more than 230 fish populations reveal that there is a median reduction of 83% in their breeding population size from known historic levels (Hutchinson and Reynolds). Scientists estimate that we're now losing species at 1,000 to 10,000 times the background rate, with literally dozens going extinct every day (Chivian and Bernstein). As many as 30 to 50% of all species are possibly heading toward extinction by midcentury (Thomas et al. 145-148). This would be a scary future, indeed.

If we want to stay alive, if we believe in the rights of other species to exist, and the rights of Mother Earth, our impact on the planet has to be reduced. This is not an issue concerning a country, an ethnic group, a religion or even humans only. It is our problem; it concerns all living beings.

The root cause of this devastation, this debacle, this collapse is an economy that is based on the exploitation of nature and other fellow humans, competition, growth, consumption, and profit maximization. Thus, we must seek the root cause of the environmental crisis in the dominant socio-economic paradigm we live in (Figure 2). Professor Guy McPherson from the School of Natural Resources at University of Arizona puts the existing dominant paradigm's contradictions right in our face: "If you think the economy is more important than the environment, try holding your breath while counting your money" (Komlik).

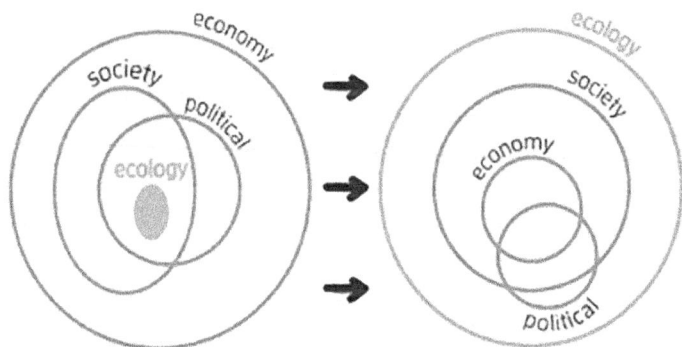

Figure 2: *Shifting the dominant socio-economic paradigm.*

It is obvious that humanity cannot continue with the mode of existence we have outlined so far on the planet. This existing dominant paradigm is not sustainable. Like James Lovelock suggests in the Gaia Hypothesis, if our planet is a synergetic and self-regulating system that created, and now maintains, the climate and biochemical conditions that make life on Earth possible, she may get rid of us, and *Homo sapiens* will soon take its place in the fossil record (Lovelock and Margulis; Lovelock).

The Ecological Cost of Consumption

Today when we spend 1 USD on average in a low-income country, we emit 1.011 kg of carbon dioxide equivalent; whereas, we emit 0.583 kg in a high-income country (Caron and Fally, 2). Essentially, we destroy the environment with every dollar we spend. When we decide to be part of the killing of an animal and purchase 1 kg of meat, we also emit 28.7 kg of carbon dioxide equivalent and produce 4 kg of waste. When we buy a pair of trousers, we emit 6.3 kg of carbon dioxide equivalent and produce 25 kg of waste. Every time we renew our smart phone because of planned obsolescence, we produce 110 kg of carbon dioxide equivalent and 86 kg of waste (Laurenti, 48,62). 1 kg of industrially produced meat has an unbelievable water footprint of 15,500 litres (Hoekstra 2008), 1 pair of cotton trousers 3233 to 4894 litres (Chico et al 242), and a smartphone requires 18m^2 of land and 13,000 litres of water (Burley 4, also see watercalculator.org).

Due to our economic activity, we have passed the yearly regenerative capacity of the Earth starting in the 1980s. In 2017, World Overshoot Day[3] was 1st of August. Unfortunately, as the consumer economy continued to grow further, the overshoot took place even earlier in the following years. In 2018 and 2019, the overshoot worsened and took place on the 28th and 29th of July respectively. In 2020, as a result of the closures that took place in the first six months of the year due to Covid 19, the overshoot got relatively better and moved back to August 22nd ("Past Earth Overshoot Days"). However, when the closures due to the pandemic ended, it unfortunately started to worsen again and Overshoot Day took place earlier in the year, on

---

3   World Overshoot Day gives the date in a year where humankind's consumption of Earth's resources surpasses the Earth's capacity to regenerate those resources that year.

July 30th, 2021 and July 28th, 2022[4] ("Past Earth Overshoot Days"). It is obvious that the consumption of the planet decreased when the pandemic slowed the economy. This decrease clearly shows the relationship between the current consumer economy and the planet becoming uninhabitable for living beings.

The Social Cost of Consumption

For humanity, things are also in disarray. There is a constant state of crisis. With its focus on growth and profit maximization, the consumer economy fuels social injustice. The pressure to reduce the cost of production leads to social dumping[5], slave or child labour, and inhumane working conditions. For example, in the clothing industry, companies employ their workers in inhumane conditions and with unfair wages in order to enable mass production of every new trend–and to achieve this as profitably as possible. The fact that occupational safety was ignored in favor of profit in the textile industry showed itself quite strongly in the work "accident" that killed 1134 workers in Bangladesh in 2013 (Prentice 5).

Similarly, the fact that the world's wealth is concentrated in the hands of only a few people shows that wealth is not distributed fairly in the current economic system. According to the 2021 Credit Suisse Global Wealth Report, one percent of the world's wealthiest, who have a net worth of more than $1 million, owns 45.8% of the world's wealth (17). On the other hand, 55% of the world's population, who have a wealth of more than 10,000 USD, owns only 1.3% of the world's wealth (Credit Suisse Research Institute 17). This immense inequality in the distribution of wealth demonstrates how unacceptable and outrageous the current economic system is.

Wealth and income inequality has been further worsened as a re-

---

[4] Please see https://www.overshootday.org/newsroom/past-earth-overshoot-days/ for the most up-to-date data on World Overshoot Day.

[5] Social dumping is "'the strategy geared towards the lowering of social standards for the sake of enhanced competitiveness. It is prompted by companies but indirectly involves their employees and/or home and host country governments, and has negative implications in the social sphere" (Bernaciak 25).

sult of the Covid-19 pandemic. As basic needs became very expensive during the pandemic, millions of people who had difficulty in sustaining their lives fell to the limit of extreme poverty, while the rich got richer (Oxfam, "Profiting"). The statistics from an Oxfam research clearly demonstrate this process of rising inequality. According to the results of this Oxfam research, during the pandemic, 573 people who were not billionaires before have reached the status of billionaire, at a rate of 1 in every 30 hours, especially those who had investments in the food and energy sector (Oxfam, "Pandemic"). Also, the wealth of the world's billionaires in 2020 has tripled from 4.4% of global GDP to 13.9% (Oxfam, "Profiting" 4).

To some people, having more billionares may not appear to be a significant problem. However, one should know that while the rich was getting even richer, 1,000,000 people fell into extreme poverty every 33 hours (Oxfam, "Profiting" 3). So, approximately, as one person who had not been a billionare becomes one, a million people fall into extreme poverty. This shows the societal cost of this economic system. With the impact of the pandemic, more than 263 million people were expected to fall to the extreme poverty line in 2022 alone, while the wealth of billionaires increased in the first 24 months of Covid-19 by more than the sum of the last 23 years (Oxfam, "Profiting" 3). Furthermore, Oxfam's research also shows that during the pandemic, the companies in the energy, food, and pharmaceutical industries have made record high profits; whereas, their workers' wages have stayed virtually unchanged (Oxfam, "Profiting" 6-8). This finding also reveals that companies are exposing their workers to price increases on basic necessities.

According to Bucher "This rising wealth and rising poverty are two sides of the same coin, proof that our economic system is functioning exactly how the rich and powerful designed it to" (Oxfam, "Pandemic"). This result, created by the dynamics of the profit-maximisation-oriented consumer economy, causes millions of people to become impoverished and even some to starve to death.

According to another striking statistic, the ten richest people in the world have more wealth than the 3.1 billion people who are at the bottom of the world's wealth distribution (Oxfam, "Profiting"

4). This is one of the many pieces of evidence that the current economic system we are in is not just. Also, according to the data in the same report, since 1995, the top 1% of the world wealth pyramid has increased its wealth by nearly a factor of 20, more than the 50% of the population at the bottom of the wealth pyramid (Oxfam, "Inequality" 7). These statistics may not be viewed as a problem if one disregards the impact of wealth inequality. So, one should bear in mind that at least one person dies every 4 seconds due to wealth inequality (Oxfam, "Inequality" 7). As we demonstrated with the studies above, this economic system is based on unjust dynamics and fuels wealth inequality. Oxfam describes this disparity between the rich and the poor, which has reached to extreme limits, as "killing inequality" (Oxfam, "Inequality"). According to Bucher: "This grotesque inequality is breaking the bonds that hold us together as humanity. It is divisive, corrosive, and dangerous. This is inequality that literally kills" (Oxfam, "Inequality").

This huge gap in the global distribution of wealth is an important proof that the consumer economy is causing results that are far from just and fuelling the socio-economic hierarchy. Therefore, we need a new, ecology-based economy that meets the needs of the planet. In order for this economy to meet the needs of people, it must also be built on social justice. In an inclusive economy, the production of goods and services is optimized to meet the expectations of, and to create opportunities for, all segments of society. In this economy, competition is not seen as a necessity, but as a disease of society; reciprocity, reinforcing and supportive cycles are sought, win-win scenarios are created, losses are either compensated or are given a new function. Nature is seen as a being, not a resource.

Demands for Change

A sustainable future is not possible without changing the existing dominant socio-economic paradigm based on competition, growth, consumption, and profit maximization. This sustainable future we seek should not be limited to the economic definition of "development that meets the needs of the present without compromising the ability of future generations to meet their own needs," but should go beyond this definition. The generational equity approach is fair, but our focus cannot be on development. Considering that both economy and ecology share the same "oikos" root[6], we should shape the world according to ecology, not economy.

Social norms and laws need to be constructed based on the science of ecology. As a result, in this new oikos-centered paradigm, ecology is hosting the society and the society's policies. Ecology determines the limits of the economy and the politics in governing the society. In this sense, the new paradigm and what we are looking for is transformative (Hopwood et al. 38-52) and has the goal of a "great transformation" (Raskin).

The demand for a new economy is already present and increasing day by day. In developed countries, the market for organic, locally produced goods and renewables is growing strongly. Sales of local edible farm products in 2017 totalled $11.8 billion, or 3 percent of all agricultural sales in 2017, up from $8.7 billion in 2015, outpacing the growth of USA's total food and beverage sales (Martinez). The number of farmers markets in the United States has grown

---

6   The etymology of the words "ecology" and "economy" comes from "oikos," the house and its garden in ancient Greek.

steadily from just under 2,000 in 1994 to more than 8,600 markets (Farmers Market Coalition).

According to 2010 statistics, there were 37 million hectares of agricultural land in organic production, managed by 1.6 million certified producers. Although no data exists for non-certified producers, the size is estimated to be many times this figure (Dittrich). In 2016, the total certified land in organic agriculture reached 57.8 million hectares (Willer and Lernaud 14). In 2019, organic area used reached 107.4 million hectares; in other words 1.5% of the world's agricultural land is used for organic farming (Willer and Lernaud 22, 41). In 2003, 25 billion US dollars worth of organic products were sold globally which rose up to 50.9 billion US dollars in 2008, and 90 billion US dollars in 2016 (Willer and Lernaud 26). In 2019, global organic food sales reached more than 106 billion Euros (Willer and Lernaud 22). As it can be seen from the aforementioned statistics, the demand and supply are steadily increasing.

In fact, during the past two decades, the search for a new economy was primarily focused on local food systems. The Covid-19 pandemic further increased the public policy discussions on US food accessibility, affordability, and supply chains since the local food systems became more visible and accessible. As a consequence of their proximate, short supply chains, local and regional food systems (LRFS) can be characterized as "nimble" and "connected" and necessitate an economy consisting largely of local enterprises (Thilmany et al. 87).

A consciousness is developing about products that damage the environment, human health, and the producer itself. Albeit still an individualistic act, there is a wave of conscious consumerism. People are trying to buy local, fair trade and organic products. For example in Germany 84% of people regardless of age group would like to know whether the product was fair, 82% whether it is produced in an environmentally friendly way, 81% without Genetically Modified Organisms (GMO), and 79% would like a government-enforced animal welfare label (BMEL 12).

In addition to the food sector, there is a rapid transformation in the energy sector, as well. The European Union has a target to cover 20% of its energy needs with renewable energy resources by 2020 and 50% by 2050. Ntanos et al. showed that renewable energy investment is correlated with increased gross domestic product (GDP) growth and labour force in Europe (1). Annual investment in renewable power and fuels was 274 billion USD in 2016, and 279.8 billion USD in 2017 globally (REN21, "Renewables 2018" 19). As solar energy (photovoltaic) grew 30% in 2017 compared to the previous year and reached 402 GW (REN21, "Renewables 2018" 19), while in 2021 it reached 942 GW with a 23% growth compared to 2020 (REN21, "Renewables 2022" 50). Share of renewable energy in the EU went up to 18.0% in 2018 where twelve member states have reached a share equal to or above their 2020 target (Eurostat, "Renewable Energy in the EU" 1). In 2020, the share of renewable energy in the EU reached 22.1%, and 29 EU member countries achieved a share equal to or above their 2020 targets (Eurostat, "Renewable Energy Statistics"). The positive change in the energy sector has accelerated so much that as we write the numbers are increasing.

The shift towards ecologically conscious consumer behaviour is also not limited to the US and Europe. For example, Indian consumers are also increasingly becoming ecologically concerned in their buying behaviour as shown in the research examining their pro-environmental consumer behaviour (Taufique and Vaithianathan).

We can see that there is a return to what is deemed natural, yet living by these ecological and social principles is still complex in terms of finding and trusting products and producers. The demand side, "conscious consumers," and the supply side, "conscious producers," remain largely unorganized. They accept the competition in the market as a norm and cannot think outside of the "competition is good for us" paradigm. By consequence, most people feel helpless when it comes to facing environmental issues…

However, the new generation currently between 19 and 35 years of age, accounting for 27% of the global population or about 2 billion people, are quickly becoming the world's most important generational cohort for consumer spending growth, sourcing of employees, and overall economic prospects. They are different from previous generations in driving a collaborative economy, leading the way in terms of embracing (or at least experimenting with) new formats such as crowdfunding and peer to peer transactions. The young generation chooses significantly more ecological products and are more active than other groups on environmental issues, because they have limitless ability to use technology to communicate and exchange information.

The social networks that young people are involved in tend to dominate their perceptions. This reinforces their personal emotional response and their ecological knowledge, so young people have significantly greener intentions (Kachanapibul et al.). Change is happening, and it is driven by people, especially young people, who want to "consume" better for the health of the planet and the communities to which they belong. So, we see the demand for a new economy coming from the grassroots.

Surveys show that 36% of millennials are willing to buy eco-friendly products and demand a more environmentally responsible workplace (Rogers; Guevarra). In addition to the millennials, "Gen Z" has even more significant concerns regarding environmental issues, as confirmed by the 2021 Pew Research report (Pew Research Center). Also, the survey conducted by First Insight in 2019 found that a "vast majority of Generation Z shoppers prefer to buy sustainable brands, and they are most willing to spend 10 percent or more on sustainable products" (First Insight). Compared to millennials, Generation Z are the most likely to make purchase decisions based on values and personal, social, and environmental principles. They like to purchase upcycled products; when giving gifts, they are most likely to purchase sustainable ones and return the ones that are not sustainable.

Oversimplifying a population's behaviour by dividing them into generations is rightly criticized; in fact, the First Insight survey also found that in all generations, recommerce[7] is growing in popularity, and all generations expect retailers and brands to become more sustainable. However, it is evident that young people have significantly more green intentions, choose significantly more ecological products, and they are more active than other groups on environmental issues due to their ability to use boundless technology to communicate and exchange information.

---

7   Recommerce is the purchasing and selling of pre-owned goods.

Reform and Change Efforts

As people and institutions realize the day when the Earth will get rid of us is getting closer, they are rolling up their sleeves to find a solution. Detailed laws were enacted; international agreements were made; carbon dioxide emissions are trying to be controlled with policies such as "cap-and-trade;" investments were made in renewable energy sources, and many similar steps were taken. The increasing demands for change are important accelerators leading to these developments. In this chapter, we will examine some other solution efforts that have made an impact. These efforts differ from each other in terms of their perspectives on the situation. For example, while the first three solutions (technological solutions, corporate social responsibility, and the polluter pays principle) are designed to work within the current dominant economic system, the next seven solution proposals question the existing system.

Seeking a Technological Fix

The conveniences created by technological developments in our daily lives (washing machines, vacuum cleaners, cars, etc.) create the illusion that we can also solve complex issues like the climate and biodiversity crises created by humanity with similar technological developments. Technological optimists may indeed want us to believe that all these problems can be solved with human creativity, science, and technology. But we've already seen that relying on this kind of arrogance that humans can interfere with the planet's systems by just using some technology will eventually bring us more trouble. Whales dying with 29 kg of plastic in their stomachs, or dead albatross carcasses filled with plastic on remote islands, or even mammals dying from the plastic they ate in deep forests that are uninhabited are a few examples of the consequences. What about giant plastic garbage islands in the Western and Eastern Pacific Ocean, a 19 by 5 km plastic island floating in the Caribbean Sea, and, finally, microplastics in human blood, urine, and milk? Chernobyl, Fukushima, DDT, and other persistent organic pollutants and recent crises of bee-killing neonicotinoid and cancer-causing glyphosate. Plastic, DDT, glyphosate, neonicotinoids… have these technologies been the solution to our problems?

Similarly, "green growth," a technological solution with social and economic dimensions, is proposed. However, "green growth" has been criticised for focusing primarily on large-scale technological solutions, paying little attention to politics and human rights, and failing to recognise social factors (Fatheuer et al.). For example, in the Democratic Republic of the Congo today, more than 10,000 children work in cobalt mines in horrible conditions for the electric car and electronic battery industry (Walt).

As we can see from these examples, technological development and "green growth" will not prevent the collapse of humanity. Even though technological developments can help to mitigate the ecological damage caused by humanity (machines using less, local and renewable energy, studies on the optimisation of solar panels, etc.), it is not realistic to expect solving the existing crisis immediately with a technological development. Neither solar panels nor wind turbines will save us by themselves. Technological development cannot be a solution by itself, but it can be a contributing factor in social transformation.

Corporate Social Responsibility

The concept of Corporate Social Responsibility (CSR) first emerged in the early 1930s. It could also be argued that philanthropy before the 20th century is an earlier version of CSR (Carroll 19-46). Before the 1900s, corporate donations were perceived as squandering shareholders' assets or money without their approval (Carroll 19-

46). In the case of the West Cork Railway Company in Great Britain in 1883, the company wanted to compensate its laid-off employees. Lord Justice Byron decided that the Board's job was to spend money for the benefit of the company and not for charity, and the compensation was not paid (Carroll). From the 1930s onwards, companies were recognised as institutions with social responsibilities (Carroll). For example, in 1939 M. Clark wrote *Social Control of Business* and in 1940 Theodore Krepp wrote *Measurement of the Social Performance of Business* (Carroll).

According to Patrick Murphy, CSR has four periods (Carroll 19-46):

1. Philanthropy period: Companies that donate mostly to charities (before 1950s)

2. Awareness period: Greater recognition of general corporate responsibility and participation in community affairs (1953 – 1967)

3. Problem period: Companies focusing on issues such as racial discrimination, environmental pollution (1968-1973)

4. Sensitivity period: Companies begin to take steps to address CSR, such as examining corporate impacts, changing boards, announcing social performances (1974 –1978, to date)

Today, companies care about CSR more than ever before. For example, Blackrock, one of the world's largest asset management companies, said climate change will be an important part of its investment strategy. In this context, it will no longer invest in companies that generate more than 25% of their income from coal. Goldman Sachs announced that the company will spend 750 billion USD in sustainable finance over the next 10 years. The emerging concept of "Sustainable Finance" now considers environmental, social and governance (ESG) factors while making decisions (European Commission, "Overview").

Although all this may sound good, there are a few questions. How can we be sure of the sincerity of these charitable acts of companies? What if, as in the examples we mentioned above, CSR is applied to benefit public relations and make the company more attractive to investors? Or worse, if CSR is used as a superficial compensation to cover up injustices?

Imagine a coal company that pollutes the air and then provides grants for lung disease research and cures. Such hypocrisy is common among companies, but it is sometimes made invisible by manipulation or cover-up. CSR is not an effective way for companies to benefit society. On the contrary, it is extremely open to abuse by companies.

In brief, CSR has served society for a long time. But now it is abused by some companies, used for greenwashing and other laundering methods. The fact that we have to question whether CSR is sincere or manipulative is an indication that a different solution is necessary besides CSR. Many cynical people say that CSR exists because of profitability; there's no need to get cynical because these companies simply wouldn't exist today if CSR wasn't profitable. Similarly, in our opinion, if a company isn't benefiting people or the planet, profitable or not, it shouldn't exist.

Polluter Pays Principle

Another environmental reform movement is the Polluter Pays Principle. One of the main principles of the 1992 Rio Declaration was that those who cause pollution must pay the price. This price paid was expected to prevent or reduce the damage to the environment, environmental pollution, and human health. In fact, this principle, in essence, is an environmental economics policy tool.

The polluter pays principle dates back to 1972, when it was proposed by the Organisation for Economic Co-operation and Development (OECD). Later, in 1974, the principle was re-approved by the OECD (European Commission, "The Polluter" 3). The European Union took into account the OECD's proposal and adopted this policy tool into the Environmental Action Program (1973–1976) and in 1987 included it in Article 191(2) of the Treaty of the European Communities (European Commission, "The Polluter" 3).

In 1992, 16 principles were determined in the UN Declaration on Environment and Development (European Commission, "The Polluter" 5). In the 1992 Rio Declaration, the Polluter Pays Principle was defined as a pollution prevention and control measure and was included in the list of measures. Today, it is considered more broadly as being held liable for the damage caused. In other words, if the environment is damaged, the polluter is liable to pay the costs of the damage. Today, the understanding of producer responsibility is also broader. Environmental pollution control no longer just means control at the source. It has been expanded to cover the impact of the product throughout its life cycle (European Commission, "The Polluter" 5).

The polluter pays principle inherently assumes that by making the polluter pay, if the cost is greater than the benefit of polluting, the polluting company will reduce the pollution caused. The aim is making it riskier for the company to pollute the environment by making the polluter pay a price. Otherwise, the company will have to pay for preventive measures. The polluter will have to pay the price when environmental damage takes place.

The polluter is also responsible for the risk of pollution, even if environmental pollution has not occurred yet, as well as the existing pollution. For example, in the case of the 2008 Erika accident, the European Court of Justice ruled that the hydrocarbon producer was responsible for the damage that took place at the sea. On the other hand, the user of the product indirectly paid for the price of pollution with the increase in product prices (European Commission, "The Polluter" 10). Some countries such as India, Taiwan, Malaysia, Chile, and South Africa hold the government responsible for compensating the victims. The polluter pays back the money to the government afterwards (Luppi et al.).

There are three types of instruments to implement the polluter pays principle (European Commission, "The Polluter" 16).
1. Command and control law: licensing, bans, emission limit values, etc.
2. Market-based instruments: taxes, liability rules, subsidies, etc.

3. Flexible law: environmental management systems (ISO 1401), voluntary agreements, labeling, etc.

Although the polluter pays principle is a powerful mechanism that tries to minimise environmental damage, it has some disadvantages in its implementation. First, it is unfair for the product user to bear the brunt of environmental pollution costs that are reflected in the price of the product. In this way, the consumer pays instead of the producer and the user pays through the extra fees that companies reflect on their prices, and, thus, the principle becomes ineffective. Companies can pollute the environment without any significant economic effect on their financials. With such a decrease in deterrence, companies continue to destroy the world with their actions that are harmful to the environment.

Secondly, there is a time lapse between the court decision and the environmental pollution event taking place where the court decision is made later. This delay in the law process weakens the effect of the polluter pays principle since the reflections of the damage lose their effect by the time the court decision is made. This again shows that this principle is not enough to prevent companies from taking environmentally harmful actions.

Thirdly, the polluter pays principle does not create a deterrent for companies in places where there are no strong legal institutions. This causes companies to relocate to areas where laws are looser. In other words, the polluter pays principle only changes the location of the damage instead of preventing companies from harming nature.

Besides the problems in its implementation, the polluter pays principle also poses an ethical problem as it commodifies ecological damage as an asset that can be traded and can be priced with a price tag. One of the most important paradigm changes that should take place so that humanity can evolve into being in a harmonious existence with this planet is that ecological systems should be considered as beings with rights like us, rather than as commodities.

Value-Based Approach - Creating Value for Stakeholders

According to Milton Friedman's shareholder theory, in a capitalist economy, companies should maximise their value for their shareholders by generating sustained profits and growth (Ferrero et al.). His theory proposed that the company's only social responsibility was to increase its profits. This method is known as the "shareholder business model" (Ferrero et al.). This shareholder theory has been accepted in the business world for many years. Unfortunately, there are still those who take this theory as given.

However, in recent years, the idea of creating benefits for broader stakeholders, rather than solely the shareholders, has emerged in the business world. According to Edward Freeman's stakeholder theory, a company's stakeholders are everyone affected by that company – customers, employees, shareholders, suppliers, environmental groups, local communities, etc. (Freeman). In his book titled *Strategic Management: A Stakeholder Approach*, Freeman defines stakeholders as those who influence the organisation to achieve its purpose or those that are affected by it. According to this theory, the corporate environment is an ecosystem where all stakeholders ought to be satisfied with the long-term success and sustainability of the company.

In the last 30 years, extensive academic studies have been carried out on creating stakeholder value. In *Reviewing the Stakeholder Value Creation Literature: Towards a Sustainability Approach*, Tapaninaho and Kujala did a comprehensive research review of articles on stakeholder values written over the past 30 years. Most of these academic studies examine the "multiple value perspective" rather than the "economic value perspective" (Tapaninaho and Kujala). On the other hand, there is not a big difference in the number of studies focusing on "focal firm orientation" and "stakeholder orientation" (Tapaninaho and Kujala). Tapaninaho and Kujala suggest that future research should focus on:

"the dynamic, systemic, and multilevel nature of stakeholder relationships and collaboration. Moreover, a more versatile understanding of value and value creation, as well as a broader understanding of stakeholders and their needs, should be incorporated into future research. To

conclude, the conceptualization of sustainability, the normative core of sustainable business, and elaboration on the purpose and role of business regarding sustainability serve as important and interesting focus areas for future research" (3).

Furthermore, it is also argued that an important topic of focus should be expanding the concept of value by adding other types of value besides economic value in order to facilitate access to different perspectives (Argandoña). The article titled "Toward a Relational Stakeholder Theory: Attributes of Value-Creating" describes three critical characteristics of relationships that create value for stakeholders: common interests, ability to work together, and trust (Kujala et al. 13-15). These attributes are not the attributes of stakeholders, but, instead, they are the elements or the characteristics of the relationship between the stakeholders and the company (Kujala et al. 13-15). This system is different from the profit-oriented shareholder system, and it can be interpreted as a stakeholder system. In this system, everyone involved and affected by the actions of the companies is aware of the issues. By strengthening the relationship between stakeholders and the company, the value is optimised for all the organisms and beings in the ecosystem.

This approach has great potential for solving today's problems. However, since it has not been enacted or made compulsory yet, it does not have widespread adoption.

Degrowth

Degrowth is a revolutionary, self-contained movement which was first pronounced when André Gorz used the term *décroissance* (French for degrowth) in 1972. Gorz initiated a debate on degrowth by questioning, "Is the earth's balance, for which no-growth – or even degrowth – of material production is a necessary condition, compatible with the survival of the capitalist system?" (D'Alisa et al. 28). Gorz was inspired by Nicholas Georgescu-Roegen, who is referred to as the "intellectual pioneer of ecological economics and bioeconomics" for his work *Entropy Law and the Economic Process* published in 1971 (D'Alisa et al. 28).

The second wave of the degrowth movement began in France in the early 21st century. In 2002, the first international conference on degrowth, "Défaire le développement, refaire le monde," (undo growth, recreate the world) took place in Paris with 800 participants where the degrowth movement activists of Lyon and the academic world came together (D'Alisa et al. 29). Since then, the amount of research on degrowth has expanded enormously, and degrowth has become a subject taught in the universities (D'Alisa et al. 29).

According to Demaria et al. (210), degrowth is more than an economic concept:

"It brings together a heterogeneous group of actors who focus on housing and urban planning, financial issues and alternative money systems, agroecology and food systems, international trade, climate justice, children's education and domestic work, meaningful employment and cooperatives, as well as transport and alternative energy systems. We have argued that degrowth could complement and reinforce these topic areas, functioning as a connecting thread (i.e. a platform for a network of networks)."

Governments have preferred to focus on sustainable growth rather than degrowth so far in order to avoid the presumably adverse economic and political implications of degrowth. However, since resources are limited in the world, "sustainable growth" also has a limit. This means that "sustainable growth" is actually a self-contradictory concept.

The researchers, who are aware of the fact that the resources of the world are limited, are continuing to work on developing integrated ecological-economic models to simulate the effect of degrowth. For example, Peter A. Victor analysed such a degrowth model in his book named *Managing Without Growth: Slower by Design, Not Disaster* (Kallis et al. 299). Researchers are concluding from the results of their models that although implementation of a degrowth strategy may seem like a utopia to some economists and politicians, a well-planned transition to this model may be a good solution to the current sustainability problems in our world (Kallis et al.).

Degrowth defines itself as striving for a good life for all and a slowdown of throughput while creating well-being and conviviality (Kallis et al. 297). Kallis et al. also argue that it is not possible to separate economic growth from resource use and believes that open, connected, and local economies should be built.

According to Demaria et al., degrowth needs to address reducing production and consumption in the Global North and getting rid of the unilateral Western development paradigm, enabling a self-determined path of social organisation in the global South, democratic decision-making for genuine political participation, social change, and an orientation towards competence rather than purely technological changes and improvements in productivity to solve ecological problems.

In their article titled "Successful Non-Growing Companies," Liesen, Dietsche, and Gebaue analysed 10 successful small and medium-sized companies (SME), which they define as Successful Non-Growing Companies (SNC), that publicly announced that they are following a no-growth policy. Although their research is conducted on a small sample size, the research results show the several characteristics of successful non-growing companies as summarised below:

- There can be many different motivations for a no-growth strategy such as work-life balance, environmental and social motivations, risk aversion, related costs of organizational structure.
- They focus on "better" rather than "bigger."
- Their key performance indicators (KPIs) measure product quality, efficiency of processes, working conditions, the social and environmental value of products, etc.
- They focus on innovation especially in the area of resource efficiency and aim to further reduce the total environmental impacts of the company.

In his work that was published in 2005, titled *Small Giants: Companies That Choose to Be Great Instead of Big*, Burlingham states the seven qualities of successful no-growth companies based on his research as follows (qtd. in Liesen et al. 9-10):

- Questioning usual measures of success,
- Refusing taking on external capital,
- Being deeply connected with their local community,
- Having close and long-term relationships with suppliers and customers,
- Creating a special work atmosphere,
- Having innovative management structures, and
- Being managed by a person that shows strong identification with the purpose of the company.

According to Burlingham, who analyzed twelve successful no-growth companies, successful no-growth companies do not prioritise maximising their profits as their primary target (qtd. in Liesen et al. 10). Instead, they are "interested in being great at what they do, creating a place to work, providing great service to customers, having great relationships with their suppliers, making great contributions to the communities they live and work in, and finding great ways to lead their lives" (qtd. in Liesen, Andrea, et al. 10).

In another study of 100 companies in 2012, White and White summarised their findings on the motivations of the no-growth company owners as follows (qtd. in Liesen, Andrea, et al. 11):

- Avoidance of risk, e.g. risk associated with investments needed to expand a business
- Maintenance of lifestyle, e.g. longer working hours and less family time when a business is expanded
- Avoidance of regulation, e.g. laws that become applicable to companies with a certain size
- Unwillingness to delegate responsibilities, e.g. unwillingness to transfer decision-making authority.

How can a firm apply the degrowth strategy? In their article titled "Why 'De-growth' Shouldn't Scare Businesses," which was published in Harvard Business Review in February 2020, Thomas Roulet and Joel Bothello explain how a company can implement the degrowth strategy. In this article, Roulet and Bothello state that despite political and corporate resistance, the degrowth movement already has been started on the consumer demand side, and suggest to large companies three strategies that they can adopt based on their research on companies leading the degrowth movement (Roulet ve Bothello):

- "Degrowth-adapted product design:" products with longer lifespans, modular or locally produced. For example, The 30 Year Sweatshirt produces sweatshirts that are high quality, durable and against fast fashion principles.

- "Value-chain repositioning:" firms delegate stakeholders certain stages of the value chain. For example, Lego launched marketplaces for trading used products.

- "Degrowth-oriented standard setting:" For example, Patagonia offers a worn-wear store where free repairs for their products as well as for other manufacturers' products are offered. Walmart, Nike and H&M asked for advice from Patagonia and they are following the trend set by Patagonia with the repair offer. Tesla, also, released some of its electric vehicle patents in 2014 to standardize the technological platform in the industry.

Increasing climate concerns are triggering a change in consumption patterns of consumers and driving degrowth. Firms should view this consumer-driven movement to degrowth as a new opportunity rather than resisting it. Businesses that respond successfully to this demand will be able to sell "better products" rather than "sell more," and they will be able to satisfy their customers while also protecting the environment. However, if consumers continue to focus on price optimisation, will companies be able to maintain their position of degrowth and produce long-lasting products under these conditions? Or how many customers can financially afford the required prices for these products? The need for a market where every company has to operate according to the degrowth principles is increasing due to the current status of the climate and the biodiversity crisis. However, the playing field is not level and there is no legal infrastructure to equalise it.

Solidarity Economy

The solidarity economy concept is another structure that is against today's company structure as it prioritises the welfare of people and environment, rather than profits and growth (Kawano). Miller defines the solidarity economy as an interconnected, comprehensive economic system that focuses on life values, rather than profit maximisation (Miller 7). According to the U.S. Solidarity Economy Network, there are five principles of the solidarity economy as stated below (Kawano 4):

- solidarity, cooperation, mutualism
- equity in all dimensions (e.g., race, ethnicity, nationality, class, and gender, etc.)
- participatory democracy
- sustainability
- pluralism

In the context of solidarity economics, "pluralism" means that there may be "multiple paths" to reach a "just and sustainable world" (Kawano 4). All of these five principles should be present in a successful implementation of solidarity economics (Kawano 4).

Today, the current economic theory is based on "*Homo economicus*" who is self-interested and competitive (Kawano 9). In other words, "*Homo economicus*" is motivated by individualism rather than the well-being of the common good, the community, and the environment. However, research highlights that human nature is not as simple as the assumption in "*Homo economicus*" and that it has both "self-serving" and "solidaristic" characteristics. In fact, Elinor Ostrom's work that won the Nobel Prize in 2009, shows that regions like forests, fishing grounds, etc. managed by their stakeholders performed better than the ones that were managed by private owners or the state. On the other hand, Ostrom also highlights that cooperative, collective systems must also address the self-interested nature of people to be resilient (Kawano 11).

In his article titled "Solidarity Economics Strategies for Building New Economies from the Bottom-Up and the Inside-Out," Miller describes the transformation from the current capitalist system to solidarity economics as an "economic independence movement" (15):

> *"This process begins not with "experts," but with concrete grassroots organizing efforts. This will not be a revolution in which the "vanguard" with the Truth takes power and then imposes a new utopia on everyone else. This is a revolution of secession from the world of both capitalists and bureaucrats—an economic independence movement. We begin with the places in which we have already achieved independence and solidarity, and we build our movements from there—revolution from the bottom-up and the inside-out."*

Some examples for solidarity economics that is present in our current lives are: "worker cooperatives," "libraries," "parks," "water fountains," "community supported agriculture," "carpooling," "no-interest loans between friends and family," "community development credit unions," "volunteer ambulance squads," etc. (Miller 9).

In the article titled "Social and Solidarity Economy: Is There a New Economy in the Making?" Utting, Van Dijk, and Mathei provide statistics on social economy size, such as (3):

- Preliminary results from the Global Census on Cooperatives of the United Nations Department of Economic and Social Affairs (UN DESA) indicates that globally there are 761,221 cooperatives and mutual associations with 813.5 million members, 6.9 million employees, 18.8 trillion USD in assets and 2.4 trillion USD in annual gross revenue.
- Mutual benefit societies provide health and social protection services to 170 million people worldwide.

- The global certified fair-trade market amounted to 4.8 billion EUR (6.4 billion USD) in 2012 (excluding Fair Trade USA sales) and involved some 1.3 million workers and farmers in 70 countries.

- In Europe, approximately two million Social and Solidarity Economics (SSE) organisations represent about 10 percent of all companies and employ over 11 million people (the equivalent of six percent of the working population of the European Union).

The solidarity economy is expanding as it provides a viable alternative to today's realities of profit-maximising companies with limited liabilities. However, this system operates in an unjust environment where financial incentives favour investments in the limited liability environment and investors can easily make huge profits. Solidarity economy faces some difficulties and limitations arising from other actors in the economy such as states, market actors, and social norms. There are also some internal challenges, such as infrastructure, participation, and members' preferences. The future of the solidarity economy depends on solving these challenges with the help of a strong, appropriate legal environment and public policy (Utting et al.).

Commons Movement and a Critique of Companies

The Commons Movement is one of the main competitors of profit maximisation when privatisation, companies and their shareholders are concerned. "Commons" are defined as products and resources that are created, valued, and shared in different ways while being used by people; in other words, it refers to essentially everything under the sky (Euler and Gauditz). The term was first used in England in 1215, when farmers were granted access to their masters' lands and forests in the "Magna Carta" (Aguiton).

Hardin wrote his article titled "The Tragedy of the Commons" in 1968, where he argued that the overuse of the commons causes environmental degradation and that communities cannot come to rational agreements on their own (Ostrom). He also argued that in order to properly achieve rational agreements, privatisation or an external agent, such as the government, would have to step in (Ostrom).

However, Elinor Ostrom (1933–2012), as we have already mentioned, proved that this is not always the case. She even stated that the privatisation efforts to prevent the tragedy of the commons led to the "tragedy of privatization" (Kim and Cho). Profit-maximisation tendencies and competition between individuals or companies harm solidarity, the commons, and, therefore, the environment (Caffentzis and Federici). For example, commercial interests have weakened scientists' ability to do research at US universities, to communicate with each other about their research, and to share information among them (Caffentzis and Federici).

Interest in commons has been increasing lately. Some institutions, such as the World Bank, are promoting research on the commons (Caffentzis and Federici). Today, the self-governing commons model is a candidate to be the "third sector" after the public and private sectors (Caffentzis and Federici).

The Commons Movement is not only an important part of the economy, but also a growing social and political movement – a new paradigm in which the competitive, profit-oriented mentality of the capitalist system is replaced by a more humane, environmentally friendly, and holistic worldview. Over-privatisation and the profit-oriented approach of the economy, whose arguments are against the commons, are the main reasons for the world's biggest problems today, including environmental problems and the disruption of collective action to achieve the common good. The prevention of finding a cure for malaria due to limitations imposed by patents on biomedical knowledge is just one example where profit comes before community benefit ("On the Commons").

Bollier says that the global Commons Movement is much stronger than the traditional movement, because its driving force is the unity of the participants and their commitment to self-government, rather than an ideology. Among the most important trends in digital commons in recent years is the cooperation in information sharing and knowledge sharing which have been initiated with the widespread use of the Internet. Wikipedia and free/open- source software programs are some examples of such successful digital programs. Bollier also highlights the shared motivation behind digital media, the willingness to co-create and to innovate without being tied to traditional markets or conditions. Additionally, he emphasises that joint networks are more efficient than traditional markets (Bollier). The motivation behind these successful partnerships in knowledge sharing and software can also be applied to other areas of the economy, such as manufacturing and resource management.

Helfrich et al., in their article titled "The Commons – Prosperity by Sharing," point out that the commons will have a justifiable future (43): "Markets, as they exist today in the commodities economy, will play a less significant role in the future, while the commons and the open communities of commoners will become the centre of life. For this, a new understanding of the market and a new understanding of management must evolve, in which the commons are not primarily the object of private acquisition, but are used, preserved and further developed for the benefit of all."

The Commons Movement is a criticism that makes it clear that, unlike today's economic system, we need an economy based on participation, decentralisation, and an understanding on resource sharing by companies, rather than the corporate, profit-maximization oriented company approach.

P2P

P2P is short for "peer to peer" and means "person to person" or "human to human." It includes the process of creating common goods through open, participatory production. The system is governed by processes with universal access through licenses such as Creative Commons, GPL, and Peer Production License. P2P incorporates inclusion, diversity and gender equality into the commons in its cultural and political designs. With these values, P2P aims to transform institutions in the context of the commons with a progressive approach, both internally and externally.

Open Cooperatives and Sustainable Livelihood movements guide P2P in examining the liberation of the workforce, care services, welfare, and people, and in building durable, transnational networks for ethical markets. They are trying to create an "open-source circular economy" to create synergies between cooperative co-production and sustainability. In order to be able to do this, they seek to show how the transition to new forms of production, management and ownership can resolve ecological and climate crises ("P2P Foundation").

Enabled by digital platforms, the peer-to-peer business model's significance is increasing in the economy as an alternative to corporate structures. In P2P computing networks, computers interact with each other where the presence of a server computer is not required, and peers are "equipotent participants" in the network (Bauwens et al.). Also, considering that there are users operating these computers in a P2P network, it can be argued that the users leverage on this technological tool that enables them to collaborate with each other in order to create value (Bauwens et al.), rather than profit.

P2P can be defined as "a mode of relationship that allows human beings to be connected and organised in networks, to collaborate, produce and share" (Bauwens et al.). In this context, the peer-to-peer economy is also known as the "collaborative economy," "collaborative consumption," and the "sharing economy" (Bellotti et al.). In capitalism, the market price is the main driver of the system; whereas in peer to peer production, the main driver is mutual coordination.

There is also a strong relationship between peer to peer systems and the commons where P2P is the enabler, creating the optimal conditions for communing. David Bollier defines the characteristics of the commons as "a shared resource, co-governed by its user community according to the rules and norms of that community" (Bauwens et al. 3). In this context, the internet is offering an efficient platform for social transformation where the roles of the market and the government are less important and the ease of "many-to-many" communication is enabling self-organisation and self-governance on a global scale (Bauwens et al.). In other words, peer to peer systems are enabling the implementation of the self-governed commons on a global scale, diminishing the role of third-party actors such as the government and private companies. Bauwens highlights the potential social transformation that can take place with the growth in P2P as follows (5):

"As a result, the emergence and scaling of these P2P dynamics point to a potential transition in the main modality by which humanity allocates resources: from a market-state system that uses hierarchical decision-making (in firms and the state) and pricing (amongst companies and consumers), towards a system that uses various mechanisms of mutual coordination. The market and the state will not disappear, but the configuration of different modalities – and the balance between them – will be radically reconfigured" (Bauwens et al. 5).

Taking one step further, according to Eisenstein, the internet is an example of a "participatory gift economy." It is a P2P network where there is no distinction between producers and consumers, and when we share information, recommendations, songs, etc. in our online network, we do not charge anyone for the information we provide, making it a gift economy.

Perceiving themselves as an ally of the commons, P2P networks are a form of resistance to institutional structures. So, it is a movement to reinvent how the business world can be different from the companies that rely on making profits for shareholders.

Social Enterprises

The European Commission defines social enterprises as social operators, whose main objective is to have a social impact rather than making a profit for their owners or shareholders (Noya and Clarence). Solidarity, focus on people rather than profits, and participative governance are the main values that should be present in social enterprises (Noya and Clarence). Social enterprises' aim is to make up for the insufficiencies of the existing economic system by offering solutions through the creation of sustainable social value and environmental protections (Bayraktar et al.).

The emergence of social enterprises as a sector was triggered by the economic recession in 1973 due to high oil prices. In those years, government funds given to non-governmental organisations in the United States were cut. An increasing number of nonprofit organisations had to compete fiercely for these funds. Faced with decreasing funds and increasing social needs, the focus of socially responsible organisations shifted. This resulted in the establishment of self-financing social enterprises (Poon).

On the other hand, the main reason for the establishment of social enterprises in Europe was to create job opportunities to cope with the high unemployment that occurred during the economic downturn. Governments supported the establishment of social enterprises and considered social enterprises as the solution partners to social problems in Europe (Poon).

Social enterprises are becoming more and more involved in the commons, contributing to the development of society, and creating value in economic activities (Meyer). In their article, "Communities and Social Enterprises in the Age of Globalization," Berkes and Davidson-Hunt say that social enterprise-based commons are successfully interacting with global actors in rural areas. The social enterprise structure ensures that rural residents are reassured about resources and decisions regarding their management (Berkes and Davidson-Hunt).

Svendsen and Ueda argue that a nonprofit run by social entrepreneurs will do better than a for-profit company run by a commercial entrepreneur for a social cause. This shows that social enterprises play an important role in protecting the global commons. Additionally, social enterprises are connecting people and making the benefits of the peer-to-peer economy more efficient (Roh).

Accordingly, business entrepreneurs measure performance in terms of profit; whereas, social entrepreneurs measure positive returns to society (Zheliazkov and Stoyanov). However, seeking to achieve social, cultural, and environmental progress does not necessarily mean that social enterprises should not be making profits

(Zheliazkov and Stoyanov). It means that they need to reinvest the profits they have made to increase sustainability and impact.

New forms of business emerge as social enterprises are organised into networks such as the Ashoka Foundation (Ashoka: "Everyone"), which brings together more than 3,500 scholars in more than 92 countries, or Good4Trust, which was founded in 2014 and brings together hundreds of social entrepreneurs (British Council). These organisations build solidarity, instead of competition. They help each other increase their social impact and reduce their ecological impact.

Transition Network

Another grassroots movement is the "Transition Network" that has come together to re-imagine and rebuild the world ("A Movement of Communities"). The communities within this network are reclaiming the economy, sparking entrepreneurship, reimagining work, re-skilling themselves, and weaving webs of connection and support. They also have a REconomy[8] line of work in exploring the potential of community-led economic change. Their aim is a future of low carbon emissions, and mutually supportive, socially just communities.

They continue their work in accordance with a set of change principles ("Transition Network Principles"). These are:

1. Respect the resource limit and ensure resilience

2. Promoting inclusion and social justice

3. Self-organised decision-making at appropriate points

4. Adapting to innovation as an experimental, learning network

5. Freely sharing power and ideas

6. Collaborate and seek synergy

---

8   According to the Transition Network, REconomy focuses on "how [we can] help ensure that our local economies support the changes we want to see in the world" ("What is REconomy").

7. Developing positive vision and fostering creativity

8. Balanced life

To further explain "balanced life," according to the Transition Network, "transition" can only be achieved when the "brain," "heart," and "hands" are in harmony. The brain represents our use of intelligence to find ways to live a better life, based on knowledge and evidence. The heart symbolises that we take care of the emotional, psychological, and social aspects of our work and operate with compassion. The hands refer to transforming our vision and ideas into a tangible reality and initiating a new and healthy economic system in the place where we live ("Transition Network Principles").

The Prosumer Economy: The Anatomy of Transformation

Whether it's a successful small or medium-sized (SME) company that identifies itself as a "slow company" or a "degrowth company," a solidarity economy cooperative, a commons institution, a P2P network, a social enterprise, or just an NGO-owned business enterprise, all these corporate entities are united under the roof of the Prosumer Economy. These legal entities are ecologically and socially fair businesses (Honeyman and Jana), whose legal basis is expressed as social enterprises or certified social aid organisations. The Prosumer Economy is in alignment with all major grassroot movements and rooted in their existing diversity and multiplicity. Therefore, wherever possible, it seeks to create synergy and integration with all movements mentioned above such as P2P, degrowth, solidarity economy, and the transition network.

We define the *Prosumer Economy* as a macroscale circular economy with positive, or minimum negative, ecological and social impact. In this economy, leakage of wealth out of the system is minimised. The Prosumer Economy is an ecosystem of producers and prosumers, who have synergistic and circular relationships with deepened circular supply chains/networks. In the Prosumer Economy, there is no waste and there are no permanent negative effects on nature and society; it is an economic ecosystem which is like a lake or like a forest – productive and collaborative. These rapidly growing and widespread networks come together with today's social and environmental reality (Özesmi, "The Prosumer").

This new economic ecosystem, namely the Prosumer Economy, creates a healthy and natural ecosystem without damaging the world. It works like a forest, contributing to biodiversity and reducing the amount of carbon in the atmosphere. This new economic order is the only way for human society to stay alive and thrive. However, for such a system to emerge, expand and cover sufficient economic volume, a legal and political environment is required that strengthens and supports new forms of company existence. For this new form of company, a new "company law" is needed that is different from the existing one. This need for a new "company law" is addressed in more detail in a forthcoming book.

The Prosumer Economy is inclusive by definition; in other words, the system design is based on inclusivity where the system circulates wealth among small-scale ecologically and socially fair producers. The Prosumer Economy creates a circular economy not only at the product or service level, but also, more importantly, at the macroscale among producers. The wealth generated within the system starts going from one hand to another, creating true economic and social development through circularity. By the time the Prosumer Economy has emerged, many grassroots movements have also emerged to establish ecological and social justice. These grassroots movements can create strong synergies and bonds with the Prosumer Economy because they share practically the same values.

Maybe the oldest and most common grassroots movement are cooperatives. Cooperatives are an essential part of the Prosumer Economy. The seven principles of cooperatives are also ones that the Prosumer Economy values:

1. Voluntary and open partnership
2. Democratic control by partners
3. Economic participation of partners
4. Autonomy and independence
5. Education, training, and informing

6. Cooperation among cooperatives

7. Concern for society

But, in a much broader framework, the Prosumer Economy shares the overarching goal of "The Social Solidarity Economy" as an alternative to capitalism and other authoritarian, state dominated economic systems ("Qu'est Ce Que l'économie"). It also aims to transform the social and economic system that include public, private, and third sectors...

The governance of the Prosumer Economy is in the hands of prosumers, who source their needs from ecologically and socially just goods and services from producers. Everyday, they vote with their wallets. When they take out their wallets and pay, they invest in a product or service. As producers also source their inputs from similar producers, they deepen the supply chain in the Prosumer Economy. Everyone becomes a prosumer. The success and wellbeing of these producers will pull popular opinion to support the sustainable alternatives. As such, producers in the consumer economy will also be pulled in. This will push the unsustainable alternatives, the ecologically and socially destructive, profit maximising, and externalising ones from the centre to the margins. Power will shift with the economy. Prosumers who are part of the modes of production will know who is producing the products and services. Knowing the producers, they will trust that just working conditions are ensured, the impacts on the environment are minimised, and everyone's health is cared for. The prosumer can verify practices as the system is based on full transparency and accountability.

Similar systems of ethics, trust, and standards have emerged from Anatolia in the past, such as "Ahilik" (Kantarcı). Ahi organisations were present in all craftsmanship and trade businesses, and ensured that there was no competition but honesty, justice, customer satisfaction, and the highest quality of production. They governed the bazaars of all cities, small and large. In the Prosumer Economy, similarly, we bring together ecologically and socially just producers and prosumers in shaping an economy based on ethics. As in a bazaar, producers are preferably small scale and local.

As in *Ahi* organisations, in line with tradition, the Grand Bazaar in Istanbul was governed by the shop owners. In modern times, this is continued through an association formed in 1952 in a legalized "nation state" environment. One could argue nation state democratic processes, or multilateral dialogue and agreements that lead to pro-environmental and prosocial legislation would be helpful in creating the aspirations of the Prosumer Economy. We might be sympathetic to such an idea, and we are happy to see it when it happens. Unfortunately, they have not worked in full; the situation we are in today speaks for itself. Although it could work under different governance regimes, today we are more concerned that these systems of legislation, policies, and incentive structures governed and implemented through the state mechanisms are perverse. This can be seen in areas such as subsidies that go into the fossil fuel industry or conventional agriculture (Myers and Kent 277). Hence, we want to go back to the attitude of a philosopher from Anatolia, Diogenes of Sinope, when it comes to state matters. Alexander the Great found Diogenes lying in the sun and asked him if he would wish anything from him. "Yes," said Diogenes, "stand a little out of my sun."

For the purposes of the Prosumer Economy, a prosumer is a person who treats others as they would like to be treated themselves (which is called the "golden rule"), hence creating value with their actions for society and the planet. They support social and ecologically just productions directly. The "other" to the prosumer is all living and non-living beings on this planet. Thus, the golden rule necessitates a harmonious existence with the planet as an element of it. To quote Defne Koryürek, one of Good4Trust's Council of Seven members in Turkey: "Prosumers are the ones who refuse the two polar definitions of the growth economy knowing that every producer is also a consumer and every consumer is a producer. Longing for a good, clean, and just civilisation, they adopt actions that will protect fauna, flora, and therefore tomorrow. They count these values as a compass in questioning the production and consumption processes." This blurring of the roles of consumers and producers is said to originate in the cooperative self-subsistence movements during economic crises going back all the way to the Great Depression starting in 1929.

In fact, "prosumer" was first defined as a specific term in 1980 (Toffler) to describe a proactive consumer, who is involved in the design and the improvement of goods and services. For us, the prosumer is the reason for the good and service. Since 1980, the term has evolved to describe consumers who consume what they produce (Paltrinieri and Esposti). An example would be a person who produces the electricity they use on their roof, through solar photovoltaic panels. The closest definition to the prosumer in the context of the Prosumer Economy is stated by Paltrinieri and Esposti (30):

> *"A commons based prosumerism may arise from the use of social media to promote civic engagement, and to build relationships based on specific interests and mutual trust, through a process in which citizenship is activated in actions of mutual support."*

As Alhashem has observed, prosumerism is a discursive practice of consumer empowerment through self-discipline and collective education, in contrast to other exploitative practices such as consumer co-creation by corporations. This approach to the Prosumer Economy is parallel to the understanding of the activists, who embrace prosumerism as a way to exclude and resist the profit-maximising corporate producer. Supporting other small and local producers may seem irrelevant to people with diminished disposable income due to various economic trends such as globalisation, automation, and wealth concentration. However, the Prosumer Economy at the local level highlights local development and solidarity. Everyone becomes a producer to make a living, hence, becoming a prosumer.

The Transition to the Prosumer Economy

We want to abandon the current mode of consumption. We want to build a Prosumer Economy. The building of the Prosumer Economy will need a transition process, from a mechanical economy that thinks it can get bigger and faster to one that is organic and homeostatic. In this shifting of conceptualisation to a Prosumer Economy, we believe that civil society and grassroots are critical in influencing and shaping political and economic decisions. If enough people, and especially young people, organise, believe in real and solid change, and act on it, the transition is possible. For this, ordinary people need to gain power, have a strong voice, connect with people who share their concerns, and act together for social change.

This grassroots conceptualisation and organisational language is immediately attributed to left movements and is labelled as socialist, or even as communist, as a reaction. Please note that the same language is also used by the right movements. These bottom-up approaches and collective action are not reserved to any ideology but are tools of social change. Prosumer Economy refuses to succumb to sides or frames or categorisations of the past; it has a meta-vision (Özesmi, "Metadisciplinarity"). Old governance systems are failing to understand that their realm does not exist anymore. Together with the youth, we need to move beyond our known paradigm and must reshape society's relationship with nature. What needs to be done in this new paradigm, which will act as a lever, is to shape the current economy.

Let's explain the transformation that will be necessary for the transition to the Prosumer Economy with the help of the following series of visuals:

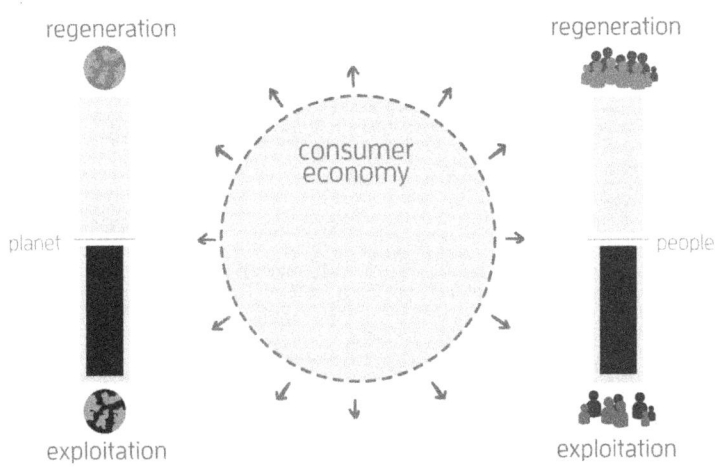

Figure 3: *The growth of the economy that is exploiting the planet and people. The economy has reached its limits, where planetary life support systems are collapsing.*

As seen in Figure 3, the economy in the current socioeconomic paradigm is a balloon that will eventually explode. It is based on the myth of the perpetual motion machine. Infinite growth in a finite world is simply against physics. In reality, the existing economic system is not a perpetual motion machine; it is a dirty and oily internal combustion engine, burning fossil fuels, spewing pollution, making human and nature deadly ill. The consequences are climate change and the biodiversity crisis. However, we don't need to succumb to our hubris. There is a way out of the climate and biodiversity crises. We can have a strong and vibrant economy to fulfil our needs and earn a livelihood. And this economy can be a completely different one.

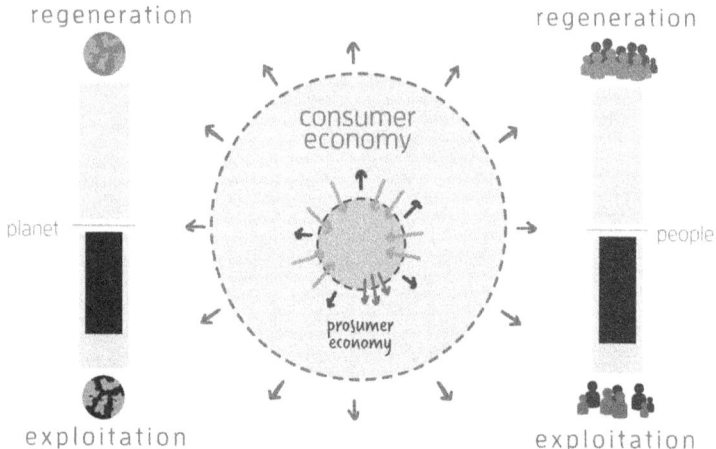

Figure 4. *A Prosumer Economy is seeded into the existing economy, and starts eating consumption through growth, and as leakage of wealth and materials to the outside of the Prosumer Economy is reduced, the consumer economy's growth will slow down.*

As seen in Figure 4, let's seed this consumer economy with a Prosumer Economy. The Prosumer Economy inside this system will grow into it, if the wealth that goes in is more than the wealth that goes out. Essentially, we are building towards creating a non-leaky system. This will reduce the overall growth of the consumer economy and hence the negative impact on people and the planet. One may visualise a bacterial growth in a petri dish to get a sense of the transformation process. As the bacteria grow in the petri dish by eating the agar, the food is transformed into more bacteria in Figure 5. Consider the consumer economy as the food of the Prosumer Economy.

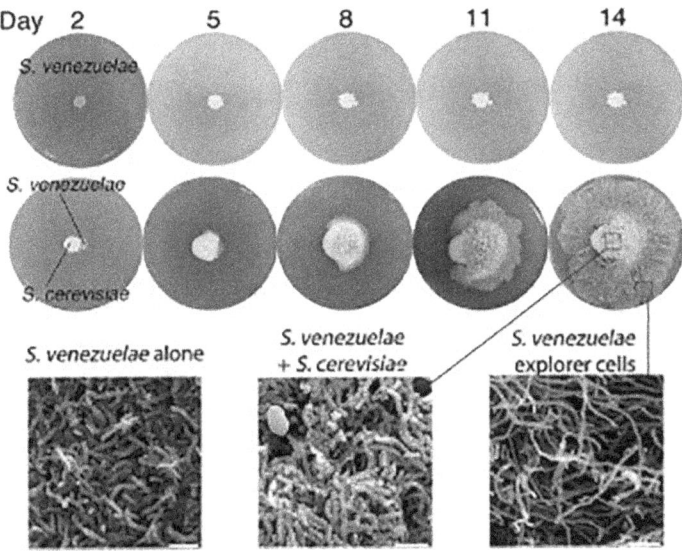

Figure 5: *Synergistic bacterial and fungal growth in a petri dish over time, transforming the agar into bacteria and fungus. Please note that synergistic cooperation between two kingdoms leads to elevated levels of transformation (Jones et al. 3).*

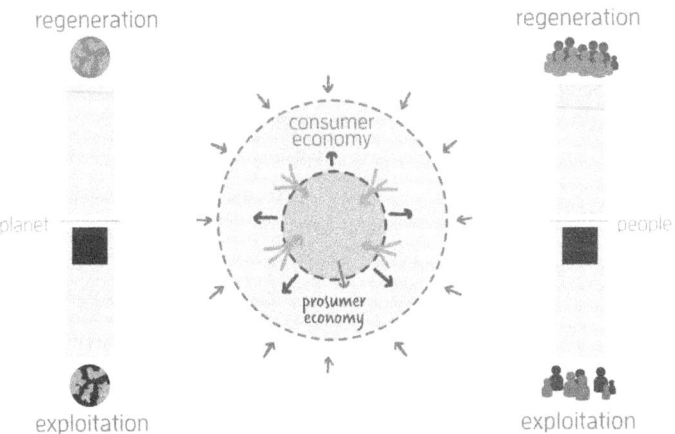

Figure 6. *As the leakage is eliminated and synergistic macroscale circular economic relations are established, the consumer economy will be consumed and will stop expanding and start shrinking.*

If we eliminate the leakage completely and start building a macro-level circular economy that does not produce waste and exploitation – in other words, eliminates externalities – not only will we be able to stop the growth of the consumer economy, but we will be able to stop the destruction of nature and exploitation of people (Figure 6). The macro-level economy is similar to the mutualism between the bacteria and the fungi (Figure 5) and is based on synergistic win-win constructions. Producers in the system will provide for each other; they will inspire each other and find purpose together.

It is an ironic myth of the current socio-economic paradigm that competition makes things "better," more "efficient," and leads to "progress." All these statements are dependent on the "for whom" context. Empirically, it does not hold true that competition, as opposed to cooperation, yields better results (Kohn). Competition is not an inevitable part of "nature" and definitely not of "human nature." In nature, which is not an ethical role model for human society, it barely exists, and is less effective than cooperation in natural selection (Kropotkin).

Regeneration After Transitioning to the Prosumer Economy

Once the Prosumer Economy becomes "the predominant economic system," essentially transforming to such a level that it encompasses the whole system, it will not only be circular but also regenerative. This transformation can meet the emotional and psychological needs of people while providing for their physical needs, creating harmony with nature. The regenerative economy will be increasing synergies, rehabilitating, and giving back to nature (Figure 7).

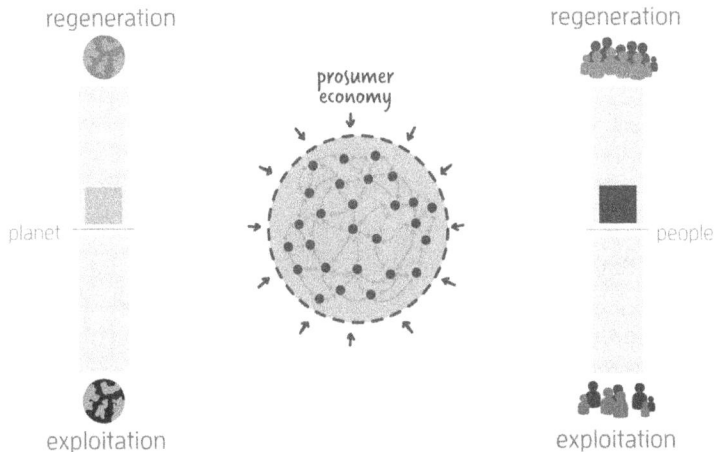

Figure 7: *When the Prosumer Economy encompasses the whole economy and, through synergistic interactions, allows for regeneration of human relations, it will enrich biodiversity and planetary life support systems.*

Being Like a Forest

In the final stage of the Prosumer Economy, imagine a forest, a meadow ecosystem, or an ecosystem like the Baikal Lake. These ecosystems are defined by physical boundaries, such as geomorphology, altitude, or climate. These are very complex ecosystems, and they are very productive. They are full of life, containing a myriad of producers and consumers, or rather prosumers.

Lake Baikal, the world's deepest and largest lake by volume, is located in the South Siberian region of Russia. At least 25 million years old, Lake Baikal is also the oldest lake in the world and was added to the UNESCO World Heritage List in 1996. Lake Baikal accounts for 20% of the world's freshwater reserves and is also rich in biodiversity. This lake ecosystem is home to many endemic species that are not found anywhere else in the world. About 80% of the more than 3,700 species found in Lake Baikal are endemic. The most famous of these endemic species is the nerpa (*Pusa sibirica*), the world's only freshwater seal (Szalay). In addition to more than

50 fish species, Lake Baikal has over 100 species of flatworms, 700 species of arthropods (insects, spiders, and crustaceans), and 170 species of mollusks. All of these invertebrates help purify the water of Lake Baikal. Lake Baikal is an ecosystem that has survived for 25 million years, which is rich in biodiversity and is based on unique cycles. If Lake Baikal can sustain such vitality, such an economy based on give-and-take interactions and circularity, why not shape our own economy like this?

Lake Baikal is no exception, let's also examine the Amazon Rainforest, which is the largest rainforest in the world. The Amazon rainforest contains 40% of the world's tropical forest size and conservatively includes at least 15,000 different tree species (Maslin et al.). Despite being 55 million years old, the Amazon Rainforest has remained as one of the world's richest and most diverse biological reservoirs, inhabited by millions of insects, plants, birds and other creatures (Maslin et al.). Home to about 390 million trees, the Amazon Rainforest is also an enormous home for biodiversity with about 2.5 million insect species and 2,000 different mammal and bird species (Müller). In addition to being home to an exceptionally rich biodiversity, the annual total economic contribution of the Amazon forests' ecosystem service was estimated to be approximately 3.527 billion in the 2007 USD price index (4.62 billion USD in 2021), which is 3.4 times more than the world's 20 most valuable companies' total income of 1.367 billion USD in 2021 (Müller; "$1 in"; Groot et al. 55).

Taking these two ecosystems into consideration, we believe that it is not impossible to create a Prosumer Economy ecosystem in the world as we described, since already many similar ecosystems exist. We can take the example of these self-sufficient ecosystems that have existed for millions of years and shape our own economic ecosystem. Our main thesis in this book is that the human economy can exist in harmony with the planet, like a forest, like a lake. We can think of the Prosumer Economy we are building as a human economic system in the structure of a forest ecosystem (Figure 8).

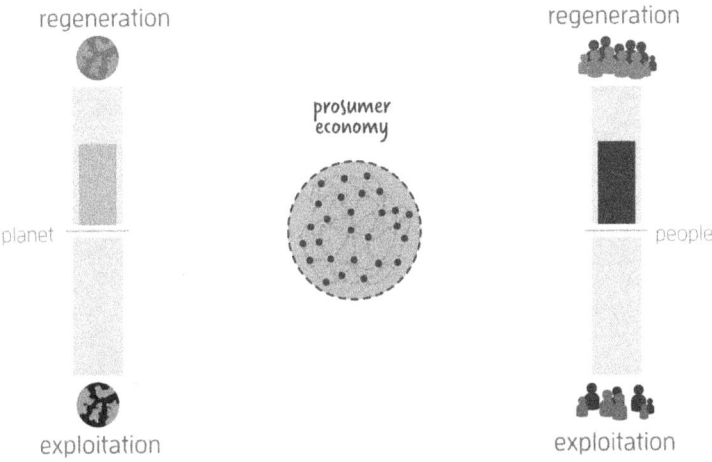

Figure 8: *The Prosumer Economy is like a forest, bound by physical planetary boundaries, the space other living beings use, and with the energy that the sun provides. A macroscale circular economy, where there is no waste and negative impact and people exist in harmony with the planet.*

Putting the Prosumer Economy into Practice: Good4Trust

We can become a forest through planting trees one by one and by knitting relations with patience and determination. Relationships are key here. Theoretically, businesses can be ecologically and socially just on their own, but the fact that individual trees do the right thing and satisfy their consciences does not necessarily contribute to the transformation of the system... For the transformation to happen, businesses should not just be "one and free like a tree" but also come together to be "sororal like a forest," to build this new ecosystem as Nazım Hikmet says in his poem (Fuat 120).

To build an economy that is "sororal like a forest," a framework is necessary. With this purpose of actualising the Prosumer Economy, we have developed a digital public utility and an integrated community called Good4Trust. Businesses and people joined the Good4Trust system one by one and became associated with each other; that is to say, they started sharing with and purchasing from each other. In a way, we are slowly but surely growing this economic ecosystem by planting tree after tree and adding squirrels, birds, ants, and insects to the ecosystem.

In this community, producers and consumers come together to be prosumers, and they support each other along their journey to create a Prosumer Economy. They establish a governance system among themselves while also collaborating to build this new circular economy at the macro-level.

The prosumer is someone who is actively involved with the design, production, and delivery of the goods and services they use. Anyone can register and become a prosumer in Good4Trust and participate in the system. We assume that the people who join this digital public utility we call Good4Trust want to lead a lifestyle based on values of goodness, and they join the platform with this purpose.

In Good4Trust, goodness is defined by the "golden rule" as written in Norman Rockwell's mosaic in the United Nations building (United Nations). In the mosaic, there are people from various nationalities and, at the bottom of the mosaic, "Do unto others as you would have them do unto you" is written in gold letters. The UN is an institution founded to foster peace, which brings 193 countries together. We believe that this rule, which is the basis for peace, is essential for peace with the planet, too.

Figure 9: *Norman Rockwell's mosaic called the "Golden Rule" (Rockwell).*

Actually the "golden rule" is not a novelty that came up in the 20th century; on the contrary, it dates back thousands of years. In fact, Confucius advised *not to treat people the way you would not want to be treated*. Also known as the "ethic of reciprocity," the golden rule has been embraced in many religions, cultures, and societies (Wattles). This principle is mentioned in Buddhism, Jainism, Islam, Sikhism, Taoism, Confucianism, Judaism, Hinduism, and Christianity (Wattles).

According to Jeffrey Wattles, the golden rule is a part of "our planet's common language, shared by persons with differing but overlapping conceptions of morality." Also, according to Wattles, "only a principle so flexible can serve as a moral ladder for all humankind."

Who are the "others" stated in the golden rule? We don't even question this. In our anthropocentric point of view, the "others" are, of course, humans. However, if we want to be in peace with the planet, the golden rule needs to extend itself to all other living, and even nonliving, beings. Bearing this in mind, in Good4Trust, the golden rule includes all beings.

Whether you are an individual or an entity such as a company, Good4Trust's golden rule has four expressions for you:

- Treat all living beings and nature as you want to be treated,
- Do not treat living beings and nature in a way that you don't want to be treated,
- Wish for all the living beings and nature as you wish for yourself,
- Understand the needs and wants of all living beings, and act accordingly.

The golden rule necessitates that the platform also has a social solidarity aspect. To create this solidarity, Good4Trust has a "good deeds stream" or "feed." Prosumers are encouraged to share their good deeds or any behaviour they see that follows the golden rule. For instance, buying products and services that minimise harm to nature and society to meet their basic needs is considered the highest form of goodness, or good deeds like providing a scholarship for the education of a child or donating to an NGO (Figure 9). They can also go to each other's profiles, thank them, and send their appreciations. While also strengthening the bonds between individuals in the system, this sharing of deeds supports prosocial behaviour.

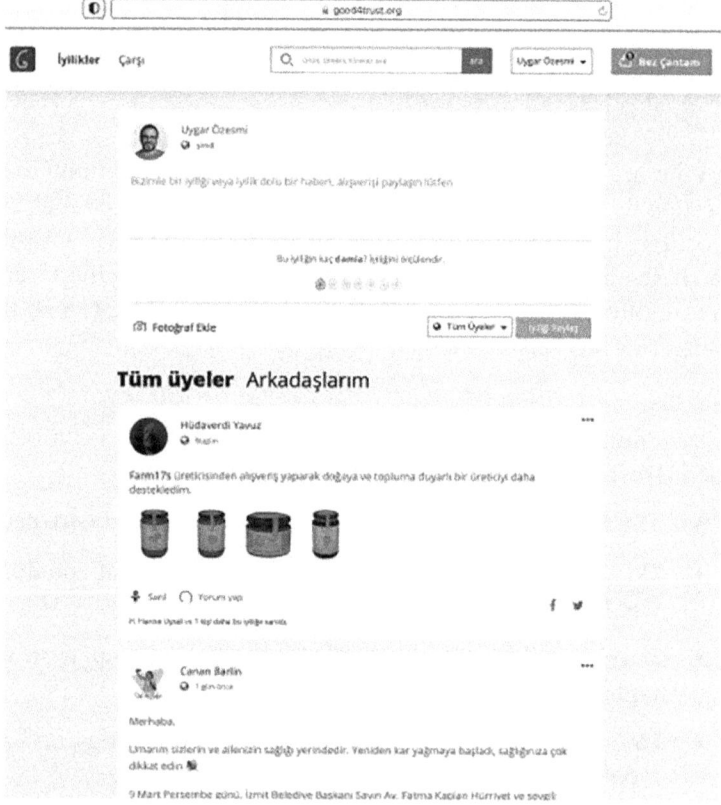

Figure 9: *Good deeds "stream" or "feed" on Good4Trust*

Scientific research shows that doing good deeds is good for your health (Whillans et al.), can be learned (Weng et al.), makes you feel good, and gives you a warm glow, a.k.a. "helper's high" (Andreoni). Therefore, the intrinsic motivational aspect of proenvironmental behaviour becomes critical for a sustainable future (Van der Linden). Studies of brain chemistry and social behaviour support this and claim that seeing a good deed of a person stimulates the desire of also doing good deeds, and this behaviour will spread and increase in frequency (Schnall et al.).

Unfortunately, we have been indoctrinated with a false assumption for as long as we can remember. We think that people are selfish and that they only act within their own interests. We know that the contrary is true, and that humans are helpful, and put their loved ones and society before themselves. Rutger Bregman's book called *Humankind: A Hopeful History* opposes the narrative of humankind being selfish and self-seeking. The examples Bregman gives are striking. For instance, he shows that the wild and selfish "real nature" of the young people described in William Golding's famous *Lord of the Flies* is truly a fiction. When we look at the real life story of a group of six young people who have been through a similar scenario and have been stranded on a deserted island, we see the opposite of the novel's fiction. The young have neither only looked after their own interests, nor have they become "savages." On the contrary, they have collaborated, looked out for each other, found solutions to conflicts, and managed to live on that island for one and a half years (Bregman).

From the striking "results" of Zimbardo's Stanford Prison Experiment to the "obedience" in Milgram's Shock Experiment, to the "violence" in Muzaffer Sherif's experiment, the stories told, though false, have had profoundly damaging social consequences. Even though it has come to light that Zimbardo prompted the guards to act harshly, and thus the evil in humanity, the "sadism" that the experiment "revealed," had no scientific validity, the "results" of the experiment are still told as if they were true (Texier; Cohen). Similarly, although it has been found that the data in Milgram's shock experiment had been tampered with and the videos of people disobeying had been hidden to a point where, although, in reality, 65%

of the participants have disobeyed, it came to the "conclusion" that the majority of the participants had obeyed the order, the findings could not prevent the conviction of "human nature" (Millard). In Muzaffer Sherif's Robber's Cave Experiment, even though he expected children from different groups to display hostile attitudes towards each other, none of these behaviours occurred in the first trial (Robinson). However, instead of concluding that humanity is not as prone to hostility as one might think, Sherif tried to hide this experiment and create another trial where he would turn children against each other with further manipulations (Robinson).

Although they are not scientifically valid and do not reflect reality, these experiments have fuelled the conviction that humanity is evil. Even though, as we have mentioned, it was later proven that the experiments' "conclusions" were not valid, the observed "hostile attitudes" are still used as an example in a book on polarisation (Erdoğan and Uyan-Semerici 18). This book, *Kutuplaşmayı Nasıl Aşarız? (How Can We Overcome Polarisation?)*, talks about how this aspect of human "nature" affects polarisation, rather than the errors in Sherif's experiment, and perhaps misleads anti-polarisation policies. Many such views of human nature based on outdated and disproven experiments still today cause us to create economic policies that spark ecological and social injustice.

Why do we continue to believe that human nature is selfish, competitive, and self-interested? The belief that there is evil in human nature is supported by the availability heuristic. As we watch the crimes committed and wars in the news every day, such atrocities become prominent in our minds; whereas, many actions and news that show the goodness of humanity remain in the background and are not even reflected on the screens let alone shared enough (Bregman). The reporting of bad events in the news is shown much more often than a favour one person does for another, not because of their actual frequency, but because it attracts more attention, because negative events have higher recall rates.

Some social enterprises aware of this have sprung up. For example, Pozy scans news and increases the visibility of good news ("pozy"). Similarly, EcoHero promotes ecologically positive behaviour and enables us to monitor our social actions ("EcoHero"). Thus, it motivates us like others to increase and reinforce our positive behaviours. Like Pozy and EcoHero, Good4Trust's good deeds stream's goal is to make the good more visible than the bad, to lift the good news and actions of people and society up.

In addition to the deeds stream, there is also a blog where a wide selection of information on Good4Trust activities are shared with the community. Examples of the content shared in the blog are case studies of the producers, festivals bringing prosumers and the producers together, information on ecology, collaboration stories, etc.

Good4Trust structures a truly ecologically and socially just economy, enabling producers to earn an income for a dignified life, as well as promoting the way all prosumers would like to live. As a transformative internet technology platform or a digital public utility, Good4Trust uses the power of people and social media to strengthen the identity of the prosumers worldwide and to support socially and ecologically just producers in their endeavours to drive an economy that is like a forest, which provides better chances for us and our planet to survive.

Governance in Good4Trust

Good4Trust's governance system differs from that of companies. It embraces community-based governance systems. According to the report "Closing Gaps in Climate Finance," written by Ashoka and Ernst & Young, governance in Good4Trust, in addition to being a nonprofit, is "what elevates Good4Trust from ethical marketplace to genuine community of trust and reciprocity" (EY and Ashoka 14).

Governance in Good4Trust is essentially based on participation and contribution. When prosumers join the platform, they are given a digital seed. This seed is watered by the "drops" of the good deeds they do, including their purchases on the platform. With every good deed the prosumers share on the platform, they can receive up to seven drops of water. Hence, every time they do a good deed or make a purchase, with the water they accumulate, the seed slowly grows to be a seedling, then a sapling, becoming a young tree, then a mature tree, a flowering tree, and finally a fruitbearing tree (Figure 10).

Figure 10: *The seven levels of participation through which a prosumer will move to gain governance rights from seed to seedling, sapling, to a young tree, then a mature tree, a flowering tree, and finally a fruitbearing tree.*

This way, through continuous use of the platform and fulfilling their needs from Good4Trust, they not only structure the economy into a Prosumer Economy, but also gain status by growing their tree. The status gives them rights to participate in the governance of the platform. As a result, the more engaged you are, the more rights you have. Good4Trust is governed by the Council of Seven, consisting of seven people who are elected among prosumers with the status of fruitbearing tree. In the selection process of the Council of Seven, young trees have one vote, and mature trees have two votes. Council candidates can only be nominated by flowering trees, from the group of fruitbearing trees. The representation of disadvantaged groups and gender identity is sought in the selection of members.

The applications of the producers, who sign a "declaration of intent" to be ecologically and socially fair, develop in this direction, and explain all production processes in a transparent manner, are forwarded to the Council of Seven. The Council of Seven evaluates the applications and those who receive a minimum of three votes are included in the system as "intentional producers;" those who get four or five votes join the community as "determined producers." Those who get six or seven votes open their shops in the bazaar as "fair producers."

The Council does not use any criteria in line with metadisciplinary thought (Özesmi, "Metadisciplinarity"). This is because of the "problem of criterion" as it was put forward by Sextus Empiricus in "Outlines of Pyrrhonism" is a major issue in the debate between the Academic Skeptics and the Stoics. What do we know? How are we to decide in any particular case whether we have knowledge? Before we can determine what we know, we must first have a method or criterion for distinguishing cases of knowledge from cases that are not knowledge. Yet, it seems that before we can determine the appropriate criterion of knowledge, we must first know which particular instances are in fact knowledge. More importantly, as Lyotard (1982) articulates, discourse that has specific rules and criteria "is always in danger of being incorporated into the programming of the social whole as a simple tool for the optimisation of its performance; this is because its desire for unitary and totalizing truth lends itself to the unitary and totalizing practice of the system's managers."

As explained at the beginning, the Council of Seven decides based on a shared sense of positive change in ecological and social impact. They look for difference in areas of inputs of raw materials, components, and all other beings such as water and energy, the production method, circularity of process and materials, workplace, working conditions, wages and rights, ethical management, communication, respect and care for human and Mother Earth's rights. The Council of Seven also has all the functions of a board by making policy decisions, monitoring progress of the platform, and holding the executive arm accountable. Functions of implementing sanctions, such as ending contracts with producers based on ethical breach and resolving disputes, also lies with the Council.

Good4Trust in Operation and Growing

This model was established in 2014 in Turkey, and it has been functioning since then. After two years, in July 2016, the online bazaar was launched and has substantially grown in terms of product variety, prosumer uptake, and sustained online activity.[9]

The online bazaar is a hub for dedicated producers and prosumers who base their principles on values of trust, transparency, justice, and peace. The system encourages circularity: money entering the system stays in the system, and the system is growing progressively. Good4Trust is maintained by a 3-7% contribution from sales, and voluntary financial support from prosumers and producers who can afford to give.

For example, the year-to-date revenue created for 512 producers by 22,773 prosumers in the system has reached 2.5 million TL as of 13 October 2022. The number of posts in the "good deeds stream/feed" is a key indicator of performance in Good4Trust. There are 8,180 deeds shared in the system. By sharing these good deeds, prosumers collected 19,766 "drops." Furthermore, approximately 48,019 "hugs," which indicate appreciation of the deed, have been shared.[10]

Moreover, with the new wholesale feature, the producers are in a stronger position to be able to supply one another's needs and keep the wealth in the system. Producers buy from each other in the offer-based wholesale system and foster the synergy in the ecosystem. At the same time, we can reduce the ecological harm that would have been caused by the transportation of purchases by retail multi-

---

9   Please see annual reports at https://good4trust.org/reports.
10   Financial and operational statistics of Good4Trust are presented real-time at https://good4trust.org/press.

ple times. Also, the efforts for the implementation of "Trust" currency by the end of 2023 continues in order to minimise the leakage out of the system and allow the wealth in the system to create circular and synergic effects. On the banknote of "Trust" money, instead of "In God we trust" on the US Dollar, it says "In Good we trust." The inscription of "In God we trust" on the US Dollar was put there to "serve as a constant reminder that the nation's political and economic fortunes were tied to its spiritual faith" after the American Civil War ("The Legislation Placing"). In the case of Good4Trust, we believe that an ecosystem in harmony with nature can only be achieved through having faith in the "good," pro-social and pro-environmental values and behaviour in humans, instead of attributing it to a higher being.

Why are we implementing local currencies? To answer that question, we need to evaluate their benefits. Local currencies stimulate local markets, enrich local people by preventing money from leaking out of the ecosystem, raise their quality of life, enable people to look out for local businesses, reduce transportation and, thus, the carbon footprint, and protect local natural beings (Özesmi, "Türkiye'de"). Furthermore, they increase collaboration between local SMEs and reduce the costs of customers through special discounts. We actually see these in our daily lives most of the time. We have buy-ten-get-one-free coffee cards, phone apps, bonuses, miles… Although these exist, they are limited to customer loyalty programs. Such programs benefit only one company, and perhaps the customer, since these programs are implemented only because they have proven their profitability for these companies. These loyalty programs can turn into even more profit for companies through the "loyal customers" they upload to their CRMs for bulk sales and marketing advantages (Özesmi, "Türkiye'de").

What we are talking about here is not a currency that profits a company or an institution. We are talking about a public service. We are talking about a currency that works exactly like the Turkish Lira but is used among people who come together in a cooperative and open to all members. So, if it is beneficial to the public, is it illegal? It is not illegal because it is a coupon that is equivalent to the Turkish Lira. Its taxes and fees can be documented and paid as if it were TL, exactly as an equivalent. Now, let's examine two local currencies that have created a significant impact (Özesmi, "Türkiye'de").

The Brixton Pound (B£) is a currency put in circulation to boost businesses and strengthen commerce in Brixton, a district in the UK. It is used by shops and businesses to complement and accompany the pound sterling, not to replace it. In addition to being conducive to the solidarity of the business owners in the Brixton market, it strengthens the pride of being from Brixton – which means the spirit of fellow citizenship. Put into circulation as paper money in 2009, the B£ became an electronic system that works with SMS in 2011. More than 250 businesses accept the B£. According to the New Economy Foundation, local currencies like the B£ are circulated in the local economy three times; thus, each 1000 B£ is circulated to create 3000 B£ of value. In this way, it raises the living standards of everyone living in the city, especially the local business owners. In addition to decreasing transportation costs by increasing the awareness and demand for locally produced goods, it reduces greenhouse gas emissions due to transportation that cause climate change. The Brixton Pound is not alone today! Bristol, Cardiff, Cornwall, Exeter, Kingston, Lewes, Liverpool, Plymouth, Stroud, Totnes, Worcester, Hackney, and Oxford have also introduced their own local currencies (Özesmi, "Türkiye'de").

Let's take a look at Switzerland. When it comes to Switzerland, talking about a bank is unavoidable. But this is not one of the banks you think of. It is the WIR Bank. WIR is the abbreviation for *Wirtschaftsring*, which means "commercial cycle" in German. WIR was founded in 1934 as a cooperative, and it became a bank later. It has 60 thousand members (17% of the businesses in Switzerland), 45 thousand of which are SMEs and 15 thousand of which are individual entrepreneurs. By shopping from each other, they create a ten-figure turnover, which is nearly 2% of Switzerland's GDP. It is accepted as the largest scaled B2B closed-circuit currency in the world. The currency, which can be converted into Swiss francs, again complements the Swiss franc. According to research conducted by economist James Stodder, the closed-circuit WIR currency ensures that SMEs are not affected as much at times of financial crisis and prevents decreases in turnover and profits. The results of this research are statistically significant even though the total turnover of WIR is only 2% of Switzerland's GDP. The value created in Swiss SMEs and sole traders rotates between them as WIR, adding more and more value to the economy (Özesmi, "Türkiye'de").

The need for the Prosumer Economy's expansion to evolve humanity's existence into one in harmony with nature and peace is apparent. Therefore, Good4Trust is currently being established in South Africa, Germany, and Chile in addition to Turkey. Good4Trust is an open-source software and is given to anyone who wants to build the system with a nonprofit social license agreement, which makes it easier for Good4Trust to increase its impact in the world (Özesmi, "Türkiye'de").

At this point, it is worth mentioning that Good4Trust, itself, is a social enterprise too. As a social enterprise, Good4Trust differs from traditional companies not only in its mission but also through its business model. Good4Trust's not-for-profit operation model is based on collaboration and encourages prosumers and certified producers to collaborate. The goal behind this is to keep the value created in the system within the system; whereas, traditional companies would prefer to take the value created in the system out of operation and transfer it into private equity. Additionally, traditional companies usually only declare the information required by regulations; whereas, Good4Trust declares its social enterprise performance in various dimensions transparently and in real-time.

Prosumers, in principle, don't consume; they purchase their needs for daily life. For example, an NGO which has built a supermarket to give excess food to ones in need (a food banking system) may buy the grocery bags it provides to beneficiaries from a social enterprise producing organic cotton bags. A prosumer buys lye (ash-water) to wash her organic fairtrade shirts. The ash-water producer sources her ash from the organic heirloom wheat bread baker, and so on. This is how the macro-level circular economy is built: with one connection, one relation at a time until it becomes a forest.

As the forest ecosystem starts forming, new scientific inquiries will also start forming. We will need researchers looking at the behaviours of prosumers and producers and compare them to that of consumers and conventional producers. The economic transactions, value chains of producers, and their supply chains and networks need to be researched, analysed, described, and quantified. We will start talking about "ecolometrics" rather than econometrics. We will see a new branch of science emerge as Economic Ecologists, rather than Ecological Economists.

The Challenges Faced by the Prosumer Economy

Like every new idea and movement, Good4Trust faces various challenges on its journey, too. One of the most important challenges is the expansion of its prosumer base. The concept of being a prosumer is not yet widespread. With that being said, we are seeing it used in different environments and more often every day. In order to spread the concepts of prosumerism and prosumers, there is a need for a paradigm shift. The precondition to this paradigm shift is the awareness of the devastation caused by today's consumption trends. Once consumers become aware of the destruction their unnecessary and/or insensitive purchases are causing to the environment, they will feel the need to change their purchasing habits. They will be more likely to buy what is necessary and they will need to buy it from socially and ecologically just producers.

Another challenge that Good4Trust should overcome is perhaps one of the most significant: the price issue. None of the price tags we see nowadays express the real cost of those products. One of the biggest problems of our times is that the price does not include harm done to the environment and society. For example, the electricity bill you pay does not include the respiratory illnesses of the people living nearby the same coal thermal power plant that gave you electricity, or intelligence losses due to mercury. Because of this, socially and ecologically just products could be more "costly" than their mass-produced and environmentally and socially expensive alternatives; however, the "cheapness" caused by such externalisation actually makes it more "expensive." Our expectation is that, with the necessary paradigm shift, consumption-oriented consumers will turn into prosumers, where they will prefer the necessary, right, and fair, instead of buying what is cheap and trendy. This, however, is a process that requires awareness building and experience – hence, time.

Another important goal is deepening the supply networks of producers in Good4Trust for the Prosumer Economy to come to life. Thus, a supply network project that links producers together and encourages them to source their raw materials from each other has been initiated to keep the value created in the system. The Mycelium Supply Network Circle, which formed in 2021, is currently working on establishing such circular supply networks where producers buy from each other in the ecologically and socially just Good4Trust ecosystem.

Good4Trust's ability to put the Prosumer Economy into life worldwide can only be possible if the prosumer-based product and service portfolio covers a larger economy than the current consumption-based economic structure. Only then can the system be regenerative and work like a forest. Good4Trust, then, would need to attract hundreds of millions or maybe billions of prosumers, and millions of producers in order to make the consumer economy obsolete. To achieve the required size to become the dominant economic structure, massive investment and/or rapid replication and network effects are needed. Alternatively, it may evolve into a movement of thousands of self-financed variants of Good4Trust-type, Prosumer Economy organisations.

As Good4Trust and the Prosumer Economy system proves itself stronger in different locales, replication will also follow. Currently there are many initiatives resisting or trying to cope with the existing economic system, which show the acute need for what we are trying to establish. The Prosumer Economy, and Good4Trust specifically, could emerge as a possible future economic model globally.

Moreover, a measurement system is needed to assess the social and ecological benefits and value Good4Trust or similar organisations create. Such a measurement system will enable Good4Trust to communicate the benefits created to society and for the environment. This demonstration could inspire more prosumers and producers to be a part of this initiative.

Is the Prosumer Economy the Future?

As we have discussed so far, the Prosumer Economy has great potential to help solve the global ecological problems we are facing. We propose a new economic governance model providing inclusive ecologically and socially just development, with the belief that it can prevent the destruction of our ecosystem and the biodiversity this planet hosts. With Good4Trust as a tool, we are not only preaching about the Prosumer Economy, but also putting it into real life. By bringing prosumers together, we are building an empowering, circular, and, eventually, regenerative economy. The redistribution of wealth to the local producers is providing them with a life of dignity and a safe commercial space. The governance system is inclusive as it is governed by the prosumers themselves. This is particularly crucial because we believe that solutions in the interest of everyone can only be achieved through grassroots governance. If we are to achieve peace and harmony with nature, then we will have to live ecologically and socially just as a society.

With Good4Trust and the Prosumer Economy, we have taken a step in that direction, and we hope to convince more people to take steps with us. At the same time, we hope that similar organisations and variants arise based on the same principles of the golden rule, ecological and social justice on a producer level, and macroscale, mostly local, circular economies with no leakage.

Now, let's imagine that the whole economy of the world is a Prosumer Economy. Let a macroscale, circular economy with positive, or minimum negative, ecological and social impact form. We now have an ecosystem of producers and prosumers who have synergetic circular relationships with deepened supply networks. The food we buy is organic, free of toxins, and healthy; we get it at a fair price. We are not concerned about harm to our loved ones, and our children's health. We personally know the people who produce our food. We are sure that the workers behind all modes of production are socially protected, are at a legal age to work, and have enough income to ensure a good education for their children. Thinking globally, imagine that we have no more concerns about the extinction of animals or other living beings. We have enough fresh water for everyone. We have a pleasant and livable climate and are not scared of extreme temperatures or storms and floods that could kill us and other beings.

We have a beautiful planet, a home called the "Earth," which we and all other beings inherited. Now, for our and every other beings' lives, we have to find harmony with our home and repair the damage we have caused.

For this, we can be a forest; we will be a forest.

REFERENCES

"$1 in 2007 → 2022 | Inflation Calculator." Official Inflation Data, Alioth Finance, 10 August 2022, https://www.officialdata.org/us/inflation/2007?amount=1. Access date 11 August 2022.

"A Movement of Communities Coming Together to Reimagine and Rebuild Our World." TransitionNetwork.Org, 2022, https://transitionnetwork.org. Access date 1 Jan 2022.

Aguiton, Christoph. "The Commons". Systemic Alternatives, 2017, https://systemicalternatives.org/2017/03/20/the-commons.

Alhashem, Mohammad Adnan. "Prosumption as a Discursive Practice of Consumer Empowerment: Integration of Individual Resources and Co-Prosumption of Value in an Online Community". Feb. 2016, https://core.ac.uk/download/pdf/83926296.pdf.

Andreoni, James. "Impure Altruism and Donations to Public Goods: A Theory of Warm-Glow Giving." The Economic Journal, vol. 100, no. 401, 1990, p. 464, https://doi.org/10.2307/2234133.

Argandoña, Antonio. "Stakeholder Theory and Value Creation." *SSRN*, University of Navarra - IESE Business School, 2011, https://papers.ssrn.com/sol3/papers.cfm?abstract_id=1947317.

"Ashoka; Everyone A Changemaker." *Ashoka Turkey*, Ashoka Turkey, www.ashoka.org/en-tr. Access date 24 July 2021.

Bador, Margot, et al. "Future Summer Mega-Heatwave and Record-Breaking Temperatures in a Warmer France Climate." *Environmental Research Letters*, vol. 12, no. 7, 2017, p. 10, https://doi.org/10.1088/1748-9326/aa751c.

Bauwens, Michel, et al. *Peer to Peer: The Commons Manifesto*. London, University of Westminster Press, 2019, www.uwestminsterpress.co.uk/site/books/m/10.16997/book33.

Bayraktar, E., Bozkurt, E., Özesmi, U.. "Sosyal Girişimin Lafzı ve Ruhu". *Optimist, Girişim, İnovasyon, Yönetim*, vol: 2, no: 17, 2014, https://drive.google.com/file/d/0Bw-DqygUWE2tZUZKMHc1RDllNmM/edit?resourcekey=0-808bw5i-hEVNt_xUbRqphbg

Bellotti, Victoria, et al. "A Muddle of Models of Motivation for Using Peer-To-Peer Economy Systems." *ACM Conference on Human Factors in Computing Systems (CHI '15)*, 2015, www.researchgate.net/publication/275653007_A_Muddle_of_Models_of_Motivation_for_Using_Peer-to-Peer_Economy_Systems/link/561efe5708aecade1acd20a7/download.

Berkes, Fikret, and Iain J. Davidson-Hunt. "Communities and Social Enterprises in the Age of Globalization." *Journal of Enterprising Communities: People and Places in the Global Economy*, vol 1, no. 3, 2007, pp. 209–221, https://doi.org/10.1108/17506200710779521.

Bernaciak, Magdalena. "Social Dumping: Political Catchphrase or Threat to Labour Standards?" *SSRN Electronic Journal*, June 2012, https://doi.org/10.2139/ssrn.2208393.

BMEL. "Deutschland, Wie Es Isst, Der BMEL-Ernährungsreport 2018." BMEL, Bundesminister für Ernährung und Landwirtschaft - BMEL, 2017, p.12, www.bmel.de/SharedDocs/Downloads/DE/Broschueren/Ernaehrungsreport2018.pdf?_blob=publicationFile&v=4#:~:text=43%20Prozent%20kochen%20so%20gut,-JAHREN%20KOCHEN%20VIEL%20UND%20GERNE.&text=MEHR%20FRAUEN%20ALS%20M%C3%84NNER%20ACHTEN%20AUF%20GESUNDE%20ERN%C3%84HRUNG.

Bollier, David. "The Commons as a Growing Global Movement | David Bollier." *News and Perspectives on Commons*, 2014, www.bollier.org/blog/commons-growing-global-movement.

Bregman, Rutger. *Humankind: A Hopeful History*. Bloomsbury Publishing PLC, 2020.

British Council. "Türkiye'de Sosyal Girişimlerin Durumu." *British Council Türkiye*, 2019, www.britishcouncil.org.tr/programmes/education/social-enterprise-research.

Brown, Patrick T., and Ken Caldeira. "Greater Future Global Warming Inferred from Earth's Recent Energy Budget." *Nature*, vol. 552, no. 7683, 2017, pp. 45–50, https://doi.org/10.1038/nature24672.

Burley, Helen. "The Land and Water Footprints of Everyday Products Mind Your Step." *Friends of the Earth*, Friends Of The Earth Trust, 2015, https://friendsoftheearth.uk/sites/default/files/downloads/mind-your-step-report-76803.pdf.

Caffentzis, G., and S. Federici. "Commons against and beyond Capitalism." *Community Development Journal*, vol. 49, no. suppl 1, 2014, pp. i92–105, https://doi.org/10.1093/cdj/bsu006.

Caron, Justin, and Thibault Fally. "Per Capita Income, Consumption Patterns, and CO2 Emissions." *Berkeley Department of Agricultural and Resource Economics*, Berkeley Rausser College of Natural Resources, August. 2020, p. 2, https://are.berkeley.edu/~fally/Papers/CO2paper.pdf.

Carroll, Archie B. "A History of Corporate Social Responsibility." *The Oxford Handbook of Corporate Social Responsibility*, 2009, pp. 19–46, https://doi.org/10.1093/oxfordhb/9780199211593.003.0002.

Chico, Daniel, et al. "A Water Footprint Assessment of a Pair of Jeans: The Influence of Agricultural Policies on the Sustainability of Consumer Products." Journal of Cleaner Production, vol. 57, 2013, pp. 238–248. ReserachGate, https://doi.org/10.1016/j.jclepro.2013.06.001.

Chivian, Eric, and Aaron Bernstein. *Sustaining Life: How Human Health Depends on Biodiversity*. Oxford University Press, 2008.

Cohen, Noam. "Beware the Epiphany-Industrial Complex." *WIRED*, 19 August 2019, www.wired.com/story/beware-the-epiphany-industrial-complex. Access date 1 August 2022.

Credit Suisse Research Institute. "Global Wealth Report 2021." *Credit Suisse*, Credit Suisse Research Institute, June 2021, www.credit-suisse.com/about-us/en/reports-research/global-wealth-report.html.

D'Alisa, Giacomo,et al. *Degrowth: A Vocabulary for a New Era.* 1st ed., New York, Routledge, 2014.

Demaria, Federico, et al. "What Is Degrowth? From an Activist Slogan to a Social Movement." *Environmental Values*, vol 22, no. 2, 2013, pp. 191–215, https://doi.org/10.3197/096327113x13581561725194.

Desai, Shweta. "Temperatures Cross 40 C in Paris for 3rd Time since 1947." *AA Environment*, Anadolu Agency, 19 July 2022, www.aa.com.tr/en/environment/temperatures-cross-40-c-in-paris-for-3rd-time-since-1947/2640960#:%7E:text=Temperatures%20in%20the%20capital%20reached,C%20on%20July%2028%2C%201947.

Dittrich, P. "Rural developement, food security and nutrition". Organic Agriculture European Commission, 2012.

"EcoHero - Be The Change and Inspiration, Track Your Eco Activities." EcoHero, https://ecohero.app. Access date 1 August 2022.

Eisenstein, Charles. *Sacred Economics: Money, Gift, and Society in the Age of Transition.* Berkeley, California, North Atlantic Books, 2011.

Erdoğan, Emre, and Pınar Uyan-Semerici. *Kutuplaşmayı Nasıl Aşarız?* İstanbul, Sena Ofset, 2022.

European Commission. "Overview of Sustainable Finance." *Finance*, European Commission, 27 August 2021, https://finance.ec.europa.eu/sustainable-finance/overview-sustainable-finance_en.

European Commission. "The Polluter Pays Principle." *European Commission*, 2012, https://ec.europa.eu/environment/legal/law/pdf/principles/2%20Polluter%20Pays%20Principle_revised.pdf.

Eurostat. "Renewable Energy in the EU in 2018." Eurostat, European Commission Eurostat, 23 Jan. 2020, https://ec.europa.eu/eurostat/documents/2995521/10335438/8-23012020-AP-EN.pdf/292cf2e5-8870-4525-7ad7-188864ba0c29. Access date 4 Dec. 2021.

Eurostat. "Renewable Energy Statistics." *Eurostat Statistics Explained*, European Commission Eurostat, July 2022, https://ec.europa.eu/eurostat/documents/2995521/10335438/8-23012020-AP-EN.pdf/292cf2e5-8870-4525-7ad7-188864ba0c29.

EY and Ashoka. "Closing Gaps in Climate Finance." EY, 2022, https://assets.ey.com/content/dam/ey-sites/ey-com/en_gl/topics/corporate-responsibility/ey-ashoka-closing-gaps-in-climate-finance.pdf.

Fang, Yuanyuan, et al. "Widespread Persistent Changes to Temperature Extremes Occurred Earlier than Predicted." *Scientific Reports*, vol. 8, no. 1, 2018, pp. 1–8, https://doi.org/10.1038/s41598-018-19288-z.

Farmers Market Coalition. "About Farmers Markets." *Farmers Market Coalition*, Farmers Market Coalition, 11 April 2017, https://farmersmarketcoalition.org/education/qanda. Access date 4 Dec. 2021.

Fatheuer, Thomas, et al. *Inside The Green Economy: Promises and Pitfalls*. Green Books, 2016.

Ferrero, Ignacio, et al. "Must Milton Friedman Embrace Stakeholder Theory?" *Business and Society Review*, vol. 119, no. 1, 2014, pp. 37–59, https://doi.org/10.1111/basr.12024.

First Insight. "The State of Consumer Spending: Gen Z Shoppers Demand Sustainable Retail." *First Insight*, First Insight Inc., 2019, www.firstinsight.com/white-papers-posts/gen-z-shoppers-demand-sustainability.

Freeman, R. Edward, and John McVea. "A Stakeholder Approach to Strategic Management." *A Stakeholder Approach to Strategic Management*, Darden Graduate School of Business Administration, 2001, https://papers.ssrn.com/sol3/papers.cfm?abstract_id=263511.

Fuat, Memet. *Çağdaş Türk Şiiri Antolojisi, Vol 1*, 17th ed., İstanbul, Adam Yayınları, 2016.

Gauditz, Leslie, and Johannes Euler. "Commons Movements: Self-Organized (Re) Production as a Social-Ecological Transformation." *Degrowth in Bewegung(En): 32 Alternative Wege Zur Sozial-Ökologischen Transformation*, Oekom Verlag, 2016, www.researchgate.net/publication/315677933_Commons_Movements_Self-organized_reproduction_as_a_social-ecological_transformation.

Golding, William. *Lord of the Flies*. Riverhead Books, 1997.

Good4Trust. "Hakkımızda - Good4Trust.org." https://good4trust.org/about. Access date 4 Dec. 2021.

Groot, Rudolf de, et al. "Global Estimates of the Value of Ecosystems and Their Services in Monetary Units." *Ecosystem Services*, vol. 1, no. 1, 2012, pp. 50–61. Elsevier, https://doi.org/10.1016/j.ecoser.2012.07.005.

Guevarra, Leslie. "Gen Y's Green Demands for the Workplace | Greenbiz." *GreenBiz*, GreenBiz Group Inc., 19 May 2010, www.greenbiz.com/article/gen-ys-green-demands-workplace. Access date 4 Oct. 2018.

Hansen, J., et al. "Target Atmospheric CO2: Where Should Humanity Aim?" *ArXiv.org*, Cornell University, 15 Oct. 2008, https://arxiv.org/abs/0804.1126. Access date 18 Nov. 2022.

Helfrich, Silke, et al. "The Commons - Prosperity by Sharing." *Heinrich Böll Stiftung*, Heinrich Böll Foundation, 2010, www.boell.de/sites/default/files/20101029_Commons_Prosperity_by_Sharing.pdf.

Hoekstra, Arjen Y. "Water for Food; the Water Footprint of Food." *Formas*, The Swedish Research Council Formas, August. 2008, p. 28, www.formas.se/download/18.462d60ec167c69393b91e03c/1549956098121/WaterforFood.pdf.

Hopwood, Bill, et al. "Sustainable Development: Mapping Different Approaches." *Sustainable Development*, vol 13, no. 1, 2005, pp.38–52, https://doi.org/10.1002/sd.244.

Hutchings, Jeffrey A., and John D. Reynolds. "Marine Fish Population Collapses: Consequences for Recovery and Extinction Risk." *BioScience*, vol. 54, no. 4, 2004, pp. 297–309, www.researchgate.net/publication/229195881_Marine_Fish_Population_Collapses_Consequences_for_Recovery_and_Extinction_Risk.

IPCC. "Global Warming of 1.5°C." IPCC, Cambridge University Press, 2018, pp. 4–10, https://doi.org/10.1017/9781009157940.001.

Jones, S. E., et al. "Streptomyces Exploration Is Triggered by Fungal Interactions and Volatile Signals." *eLife*, 2017, https://elifesciences.org/articles/21738.

Kallis, Giorgos, et al. "Research On Degrowth." *Annual Review of Environment and Resources*, vol. 43, no. 1, 2018, pp. 291–316, https://doi.org/10.1146/annurev-environ-102017-025941.

Kanchanapibul, Maturos, et al. "An Empirical Investigation of Green Purchase Behaviour among the Young Generation." *Journal of Cleaner Production*, vol 66, 2014, pp. 528–536, https://doi.org/10.1016/j.jclepro.2013.10.062.

Kantarcı, Zeynep. "An Ethical Business for Social Responsibility and Total Quality Management: Ahi Community Case." *Route Educational and Social Science Journal*, vol. 1(2), 2014, pp.177–190. *Open Academic Journals Index*, https://oaji.net/articles/2014/872-1406103604.pdf.

Kawano, Emily. "Solidarity Economy, Building an Economy for People & Planet." *Solidarity Economy Association*, Next System Project, 2018, www.solidarityeconomy.coop/wp-content/uploads/2017/06/Kawano-E.-2018_Solidarity-Economy.pdf.

Kim, Sung-Bae and Cho Sung Bong. "The Tragedy of the Privatization of the Commons". In Commons amidst Complexity and Change." *The Fifteenth Biennial Conference of the International Association for the Study of the Commons*, Indiana University, 2015, https://dlc.dlib.indiana.edu/dlc/bitstream/handle/10535/9840/Kim_Sung-Bae__Cho_Sung_Bong_Tragedy_of_the_Privatization_May8.pdf?sequence=1&isAllowed=y.

Kirk, Ashley, et al. "Europe's Record Summer of Heat and Fires – Visualised." *The Guardian*, Guardian News and Media Limited, 27 July 2022, www.theguardian.com/environment/ng-interactive/2022/jul/26/how-europe-has-been-hit-by-record-fire-damage-and-temperatures.

Kohn, A. *No Contest: The Case against Competition*. 2nd ed., Boston, New York, Houghton Mifflin Company, 1992.

Komlik, Oleg. "If You Think the Economy Is More Important than the Environment, Try Holding Your Breath While Counting Your Money." *Economic Sociology & Political Economy*, 2021, https://economicsociology.org/2014/08/20/if-you-think-the-economy-is-more-important-than-the-environment-try-holding-your-breath-while-counting-your-money. Access date 1 August 2022.

Kropotkin, Peter. *Mutual Aid: A Factor of Evolution*. Revised ed., London, William Heinemann, 1902.

Kujala, Johanna, et al. "Toward a Relational Stakeholder Theory: Attributes of Value-Creating Stakeholder Relationships." *Academy of Management Annual Meeting Proceedings*, 2016, www.researchgate.net/publication/320794709_Toward_a_Relational_Stakeholder_Theory_Attributes_of_Value-creating_Stakeholder_Relationships.

Laurenti, Rafael. *The Karma of Products: Exploring the Causality of Environmental Pressure with Causal Loop Diagram and Environmental Footprint*. 2016, pp. 48,62, www.researchgate.net/publication/301560026_The_Karma_of_Products_Exploring_the_Causality_of_Environmental_Pressure_with_Causal_Loop_Diagram_and_Environmental_Footprint.

Liesen, Andrea, et al. "Succesfull Non-Growing Companies." *SSRN Electronic Journal*, 2014, https://doi.org/10.2139/ssrn.2623920

Linden, Sander van der. "Intrinsic Motivation and Pro-Environmental Behaviour." *Nature Climate Change*, vol. 5, no. 7, 2015, pp. 612–613, https://doi.org/10.1038/nclimate2669.

Lovelock, James E., and Lynn Margulis. "Atmospheric Homeostasis by and for the Biosphere: The Gaia Hypothesis." *Tellus A: Dynamic Meteorology and Oceanography*, vol. 26, no. 1-2, 1974, pp. 2–10, https://doi.org/10.3402/tellusa.v26i1-2.9731.

Lovelock, James E. "Gaia as Seen through the Atmosphere." *Atmospheric Environment*, vol. 6, no. 8, Aug. 1972, pp. 579–580, https://doi.org/10.1016/0004-6981(72)90076-5.

Luppi, Barbara, et al. "The Rise and Fall of the Polluter-Pays Principle in Developing Countries." *International Review of Law and Economics*, vol. 32, no. 1, 2012, pp. 135–144, https://doi.org/10.1016/j.irle.2011.10.002.

Lyotard, Jean-François. The Postmodern Condition: A Report on Knowledge. University of Minnesota Press, 1982.

MacCready, Paul B., "Chapter 16 - The Case for Battery Electric Vehicles." *The Hydrogen Energy Transition Moving Toward the Post Petroleum Age in Transportation*, Academic Press, 2004, pp. 227–233.

Martinez, Stephen. "Local Food Sales Continue to Grow Through a Variety of Marketing Channels." *USDA Economic Research Service*, USDA Economic Research Servic, 4 Oct. 2021, www.ers.usda.gov/amber-waves/2021/october/local-food-sales-continue-to-grow-through-a-variety-of-marketing-channels

Maslin, Mark, et al. "New Views on an Old Forest: Assessing the Longevity, Resilience and Future of the Amazon Rainforest." Transactions of the Institute of British Geographers, vol. 30, no. 4, 2005, pp. 477–499. JSTOR, http://www.jstor.org/stable/3804509. Accessed 01 Ağustos 2022.

Meyer, Camille. "The Commons: A Model for Understanding Collective Action and Entrepreneurship in Communities." *Journal of Business Venturing*, vol. 35, no. 5, 2020, 106034, https://doi.org/10.1016/j.jbusvent.2020.106034.

MGM. "Meteoroloji Genel Müdürlüğü." *Meteoroloji Genel Müdürlüğü*, https://mgm.gov.tr/veridegerlendirme/il-ve-ilceler-istatistik.aspx. Access date 20 July 2022.

Millard, Kathryn. "Milgram Was Wrong: We Don't Obey Authority, But We Do Love Drama." *The Conversation*, 3 Feb. 2015, https://theconversation.com/milgram-was-wrong-we-dont-obey-authority-but-we-do-love-drama-36604. Access date 1 August 2022.

Miller, Ethan. "Solidarity Economics: Strategies for Building New Economies from the Bottom-up and the Inside-Out." *Socioeco.org*, Ripess Europe, Ripess Intercontinental, 2004, https://base.socioeco.org/docs/doc-7377_en.pdf.

Mohan, Vishwa. "Total Heatwave Days in 2022 over 5 Times More than Last Year's." *The Times of India*, The Times of India, 28 July 2022, https://timesofindia.indiatimes.com/india/total-heatwave-days-in-2022-over-5-times-more-than-last-years/articleshow/93172931.cms.

Müller, C. R. "Brazil and the Amazon Rainforest – Deforestation, Biodiversity and Cooperation with the EU and International Forums." *European Parliament*, 2020, www.europarl.europa.eu/RegData/etudes/IDAN/2020/648792/IPOL_IDA(2020)648792_EN.pdf.

Myers, Norman, and Jennifer Kent. *Perverse Subsidies: How Tax Dollars Can Undercut the Environment and the Economy*. Island Press, 2001.

NOAA Global Monitoring Laboratory. "Trends in Atmospheric Carbon Dioxide." NOAA Global Monitoring Laboratory, U.S. Department of Commerce, National Oceanic and Atmospheric Administration, NOAA Research, 2022, https://gml.noaa.gov/ccgg/trends.

Noya, Antonella, and Emma Clarence. *Policy Brief on Social Entrepreneurship: Entrepreneurial Activities in Europe*. European Union, OECD, 2013, www.oecd.org/cfe/leed/Social%20entrepreneurship%20policy%20brief%20EN_FINAL.pdf.

Ntanos, Stamatios, et al. "Renewable Energy and Economic Growth: Evidence from European Countries." *Sustainability*, vol. 10, no. 8, 2018, pp. 1–13, https://doi.org/10.3390/su10082626.

"On the Commons." *On The Commons*, http://www.onthecommons.org/about-commons#sthash.aigOmOH3.uxz4I8ls.dpbs. Access date Jan. 2021.

Ostrom, Elinor. *Governing The Commons - The Evolution Of Institutions For Collective Action*. Cambridge, United Kingdom, Cambridge University Press, 1990, www.actu-environnement.com/media/pdf/ostrom_1990.pdf.

Oxfam. "Inequality Kills." *Oxfam Policy & Pracitce*, Oxfam International, Jan. 2022, p. 7, https://oxfamilibrary.openrepository.com/bitstream/handle/10546/621341/bp-inequality-kills-170122-en.pdf?sequence=9.

Oxfam. "Pandemic Creates New Billionaire Every 30 Hours — Now A Million People Could Fall Into Extreme Poverty At Same Rate In 2022." *Oxfam International*, Oxfam International, 23 May 2022, www.oxfam.org/en/press-releases/pandemic-creates-new-billionaire-every-30-hours-now-million-people-could-fall.

Oxfam. "Profiting from Pain." *Oxfam International*, Oxfam International, 23 May 2022, https://oi-files-d8-prod.s3.eu-west-2.amazonaws.com/s3fs-public/2022-05/Oxfam%20Media%20Brief%20-%20EN%20-%20Profiting%20From%20Pain%2C%20Davos%202022%20Part%202.pdf.

Özesmi, Uygar. "Metadisciplinarity, Scholars, and Scholarship." *Uygar Özesmi on Environment*, 2015, https://uygarozesmi.blogspot.com/2015/12/metadisciplinarity-scholars-scholarship.html.

Özesmi, Uygar. "The Prosumer Economy Being Like a Forest." 2019. *ResearchGate*, www.researchgate.net/publication/331928283_Prosumer_Economy_Being_Like_aForest.

Özesmi, Uygar. "Türkiye'de neden yerel para birimleri yok?" *Dünya Gazetesi*, 4 July 2017, https://www.dunya.com/kose-yazisi/turkiyede-neden-yerel-para-birimleri-yok/370773. Access date 1 August 2022.

"P2P Foundation." *P2P Foundation*, 6 Sept. 2017, https://p2pfoundation.net. Access date 1 Jan. 2022.

Paltrinieri, Roberta, and Piergiorgio Esposti. "Processes of Inclusion and Exclusion in the Sphere of Prosumerism." *Future Internet*, vol. 5, no. 1, 2013, pp. 21–33, https://

doi.org/10.3390/fi5010021.

"Past Earth Overshoot Days." *Earth Overshoot Day*, Earth Overshoot Day, www.overshootday.org/newsroom/past-earth-%20overshoot-days. Access date 1 August 2022.

Pew Research Center. "Gen Z, Millennials Stand out for Climate Change Activism, Social Media Engagement with Issue." *Pew Research Center*, Pew Research Center, 2021, www.pewresearch.org/science/2021/05/26/gen-z-millennials-stand-out-for-climate-change-activism-social-media-engagement-with-issue/.

"pozy." pozy.org, https://pozy.org . Access date 1 August 2022.

Prentice, Rebecca. "Workers' Right to Compensation after Garment Factory Disasters: Making Rights a Reality." *Clean Clothes Campaign*, School of Global Studies, University of Sussex, Feb. 2018, p. 5, https://cleanclothes.org/file-repository/resources-recommended-reading-workers-right-to-compensation/view.

Poon, Daryl. "The Emergence and Development of Social Enterprise Sectors." *Social Impact Research Experience (SIRE)*, 2011, https://repository.upenn.edu/sire/8/.

"Qu'est Ce Que l'économie Sociale Solidaire?" *Réseau Intercontinental de Promotion de l'économie Sociale Solidaire*, RIPESS, http://www.ripess.org/quest-ce-que-less/quest-leconomie-sociale-solidaire. Access date 1 Jan. 2022.

Raskin, Paul. *Journey to Earthland: The Great Transition to Planetary Civilization*. 1st ed., Cambridge, M.A. A.B.D., Tellus Institute, 2016.

REN21. "Renewables 2018, Global Status Report." *REN21*, REN21, 2018, www.ren21.net/gsr-2018/chapters/chapter_01/chapter_01/#page-content.

REN21. "Renewables 2022 Global Status Report." *REN21*, REN21, 2022, www.ren21.net/wp-content/uploads/2019/05/GSR 2022_Full_Report.pdf.

"Reverse of United States One Dollar Bill, Series 2009. "https://es.m.wikipedia.org/wiki/Archivo:US_one_dollar_bill,_reverse,_series_2009.jpg. Access date 1 August 2022.

Ritchie, Hannah. "How Much of the World's Land Would We Need in Order to Feed the Global Population with the Average Diet of a given Country?" *Our World in Data*, Our World in Data, 3 Oct. 2017, https://ourworldindata.org/agricultural-land-by-global-diets.

Ritchie, Hannah, and Max Roser. "Global Land Use for Food Production." *Our World in Data*, 2019, https://ourworldindata.org/uploads/2019/11/Global-land-use-graphic-800x506.png.

Robinson, Nathan J. "The Right-Wing Story About Human Nature Is False." *Current Affairs*, 18 Nov. 2021, www.currentaffairs.org/2021/11/the-right-wing-story-about-human-nature-is-false. Access date 1 August 2022.

Rockwell, Norman. "Golden Rule." *Norman Rockwell Museum*, 1961, www.nrm.org/wp2016/wp-content/uploads/2009/04/GoldenRule-400x438.jpg.

"Rockwell's "Golden Rule.'" *Norman Rockwell Museum*, 5 Feb. 2014, www.nrm.org/2014/02/golden rule. Access date 1 August 2022.

Rogers, Gwynne. "The Rise of Generation Y in the Sustainable Marketplace." *The Guardian*, Guardian News and Media Limited, 4 Feb. 2013, www.theguardian.

com/sustainable-business/blog/rise-generation-y-sustainable-marketplace.

Roh, Tae Hyup. "The Sharing Economy: Business Cases of Social Enterprises Using Collaborative Networks." *Procedia Computer Science*, vol. 91, 2016, pp. 502–511, https://doi.org/10.1016/j.procs.2016.07.129.

Roulet, Thomas, and Joel Bothello. "Why 'De-Growth' Shouldn't Scare Businesses." *Harvard Business Review*, Harvard Business Publishing, 14 Feb. 2020, https://hbr.org/2020/02/why-de-growth-shouldnt-scare-businesses.

Schnall, Simone, et al. "Elevation Leads to Altruistic Behaviour." *Psychological Science*, vol. 21, no. 3, 2010, pp. 315–320, https://doi.org/10.1177/0956797609359882.

Stodder, James. "Complementary Credit Networks and Macroeconomic Stability: Switzerland's Wirtschaftsring." *Journal of Economic Behaviour & Organization*, vol. 72, no. 1, 2009, pp. 79–95, https://doi.org/10.1016/j.jebo.2009.06.002

Svendsen, Gert Tinggard, and Yoshifumi Ueda. ""How To Solve The Tragedy Of The Commons? Social Entrepreneurs And Global Public Goods." 2002. *ResearchGate*, www.researchgate.net/publication/5093560_How_to_Solve_the_Tragedy_of_the_Commons_-_Social_Entrepreneurs_and_Global_Public_Goods.

Szalay, Jessie. "Lake Baikal: World's Largest, Deepest Lake." *LiveScience*, 27 Jan. 2017, www.livescience.com/57653-lake-baikal-facts.html.

Tapaninaho, Riikka, and Johanna Kujala. "Reviewing the Stakeholder Value Creation Literature: Towards a Sustainability Approach." *World Sustainability Series*, 2019, pp. 3–36, https://doi.org/10.1007/978-3-030-03562-4 1.

Taufique, Khan Md. Raziuddin, and Sridhar Vaithianathan. "A Fresh Look at Understanding Green Consumer Behaviour among Young Urban Indian Consumers through the Lens of Theory of Planned Behaviour." *Journal of Cleaner Production*, vol. 183, 2018, pp. 46–55, https://doi.org/10.1016/j.jclepro.2018.02.097.

Texier, Thibault le. "Debunking the Stanford Prison Experiment." *American Psychologist*, vol. 74, no. 7, 2019, pp. 823–839, https://doi.org/10.1037/amp0000401.

"The Legislation Placing 'In God We Trust' on National Currency." History, Art and Archives, United States House of Representatives, Office of the Historian,Office of Art and Archives, Office of the Clerk, 11 July 1955, https://history.house.gov/Historical-Highlights/1951-2000/The-legislation-placing-%E2%80%9CIn-God-We-Trust%E2%80%9D-on-national-currency/#:~:text=Adding%20%E2%80%9CIn%20God%20We%20Trust,Chase%20first%20urged%20its%20use.

"The State of Consumer Spending: Gen Z Shoppers Demand Sustainable Retail." *First Insight*, 2019, https://www.firstinsight.com/white-papers-posts/gen-z-shoppers-demand-sustainability. Access date 1 Jan. 2022.

Thilmany, Dawn, et al. "Local Food Supply Chain Dynamics and Resilience during COVID –19." *Applied Economic Perspectives and Policy*, vol. 43, no. 1, 2020, p. 87, https://doi.org/10.1002/aepp.13121.

Thomas, Chris D., et al. "Extinction Risk From Climate Change." *Nature*, vol. 427, 2004, pp. 145–148, https://doi.org/10.1038/nature02121.

Toffler, Alvin. *The Third Wave*. Bantam, 1984.

"Transition Network Principles." *TransitionNetwork.Org*, 29 Nov. 2021, https://transitionnetwork.org/about-the-movement/what-is-transition/principles-2. Access date 1 Jan. 2022.

United Nations. "'Golden Rule,' Iconic Norman Rockwell Mosaic, Rededicated at UN." *UN News*, United Nations, 5 Feb. 2014, https://news.un.org/en/story/2014/02/461292#:%7E:text=Entitled%20%E2%80%9CGolden%20Rule%2C%E2%80%9D%20the,you%E2%80%9D%20inscribed%20on%20the%20surface.

Utting, Peter, et al. "Social and Solidarity Economy Is There a New Economy in the Making?" *Econstor*, United Nations Research Institute for Social Development (UNRISD), August 2014, www.econstor.eu/bitstream/10419/148793/1/862654920.pdf.

Vera, Amir. "It's so Hot, Roads Are Buckling, They're Putting Foil on a Bridge and Roofs Are Melting." *CNN Weather*, CNN Weather, 22 July 2022, https://edition.cnn.com/2022/07/21/weather/global-infrastructure-its-so-hot-extreme-heat/index.html.

Walt, Vivienne. "Blood, Sweat, and Batteries." *Fortune*, Fortune Media IP Limited, 7 June 2021, https://fortune.com/longform/blood-sweat-and-batteries.

Wattles, Jeffrey. "Understanding the Golden Rule." *Scarboro Missions*, www.scarboromissions.ca/golden-rule/understanding- the-golden-rule. Access date 1 August 2022.

Weng, Helen Y., et al. "Compassion Training Alters Altruism and Neural Responses to Suffering." *Psychological Science*, vol. 24, no. 7, 2013, pp. 1171–1180, https://doi.org/10.1177/0956797612469537.

"What Is REconomy." *Transition Network*, https://transitionnetwork.org/about-the-movement/what-is-transition/reconomy/what-is-reconomy/. Accessed 15 November 2022.

Whillans, Ashley V., et al. "Is Spending Money on Others Good for Your Heart?" *Health Psychology*, vol. 35, no. 6, 2016, pp. 574–583, https://doi.org/10.1037/hea0000332.

Willer, Helga, and Julia Lernaud, eds. "The World of Organic Agriculture Statistics and Emerging Trends 2018." *FiBL*, Research Institute of Organic Agriculture FiBL, Frick, IFOAM - Organics International, 2018, www.fibl.org/fileadmin/documents/shop/1150-organic-world-2018.pdf.

WWF, and ZSL. "Living Planet Report 2020 - Bending the Curve of Biodiversity Loss." *Global Footprint Network*, WWF, ZSL, 2020, p. 6, www.footprintnetwork.org/content/uploads/2020/09/LPR2020-Full-report-lo-res.pdf.

Xu, Yangyang, et al. "Global Warming Will Happen Faster than We Think." *Nature*, vol. 564, no. 7734, 2018, pp. 30–32, https://doi.org/10.1038/d41586-018-07586-5.

Zheliazkov, G., and K. Stoyanov. "The Social Enterprise as an Alternative Economic Model for Small and Medium-Sized Enterprises. Examples of Successful Social Enterprises." *Trakia Journal of Sciences*, vol. 13, no. Suppl.1, 2015, pp. 274–277, https://doi.org/10.15547/tjs.2015.s.01.046.

www.ingramcontent.com/pod-product-compliance
Lightning Source LLC
Chambersburg PA
CBHW031202020426
42333CB00013B/768